A WORLD
OF
TREASURE

A Collection of Short Stories
for Christian Reading

V. Ben and Nina Kendrick

REGULAR BAPTIST PRESS
1300 North Meacham Road
Post Office Box 95500
Schaumburg, Illinois 60195

Library of Congress Cataloging in Publication Data

Kendrick, V. Ben.
  A world of treasures.

  1. Christian fiction. 1. Missionary stories.
I. Kendrick, Nina, 1923-   II. Title.
PS3561.E4233W6   813'.54   82-332
ISBN 0-87227-081-5   AACR2

A WORLD OF TREASURE: A COLLECTION OF SHORT STORIES
              FOR CHRISTIAN READING

© 1981
Regular Baptist Press
Schaumburg, Illinois
Printed in U.S.A.

Lovingly dedicated to our children

Pam, Pete and Paul

Acknowledgment

To Sallie McElwain, for her typing, proofreading and other helps in preparing the manuscript.

Contents

Introduction

Some people have had such wide experience in life that they are full of stories. Dr. Ben Kendrick and his wife, Nina, are like that. Their stories, however, are not merely entertaining but are also spiritually instructive. We all tend to learn better if truth is presented attractively. Certainly that is accomplished in this book.

Ben and Nina bring the stories that are found in this book from a lifetime of worldwide ministry. They know people—all kinds of people—and it is people who make stories. Their years of service as foreign missionaries coupled with Dr. Kendrick's experience as a traveling representative for Baptist Mid-Missions have given them contact with experiences galore to share with us.

God has used the Kendricks, particularly in the lives of young people, to challenge and give guidance toward useful lives of Christian service. One of the reasons for their effectiveness lies in the fact that they are "down to earth" and know where people are. Their ability to write interesting, meaningful stories reflects that quality in their lives.

Once you begin reading you will want to continue, and you will also want to recommend the book to others.

Ernest Pickering, Th.D., Pastor
Emmanuel Baptist Church
Toledo, Ohio

Foreword

Dr. and Mrs. V. Ben Kendrick, co-authors of A WORLD OF TREASURE, have been personal friends of mine for many years. Denver Baptist Bible College, where I am president, conferred upon Rev. Kendrick an honorary doctorate in May, 1980.

Dr. Kendrick is influential. He has made a forceful impact on the great causes of worldwide missions. While he is no longer active on the foreign mission field, Brother Kendrick continues to use his influence from a position of mission executive. Greatly loved by young people everywhere who fondly call him "Uncle Ben," he also has the utmost respect of his peers who seek him out for advice.

Mrs. Kendrick, known to many of us as Nina, has had a rich background of experiences. She has been involved in such ministries as classes for women and young people, teaching in Bible school, dorm mother, station hostess, to name a few. Talented in art, writing and crafts, Nina is best described as a "unique woman."

Ben Kendrick has one of the most fertile and active minds I have known. Many new and practical ideas for the advancement of the gospel have had their birth in his "production-like" mind and existing programs which have been floundering were shifted into high gear by his motivation.

"Uncle Ben" and "Aunt Nina" are loved as second parents by many MK's (missionary kids). They are two of the hardest workers who have crossed my path. No physical or mental effort is spared in doing their God-appointed task.

When a man and wife with the above qualifications write a book, you can be sure, real sure, that it will be worth reading.

Dr. William Fusco, President
Baptist Bible College of Denver

1

EXPULSION

V. BEN KENDRICK

"**There's** a soldier at the door, George. I think he has a paper for you." Barry Vogle folded his shopping list and put it in his shirt pocket. He watched his co-worker, George Winans, as he talked with the uniformed soldier.

"Thank you, Sir." said George, taking an envelope from the government man and signing a notebook confirming receipt of the paper.

When the soldier left, George opened the official document. It was a copy of a letter from the president of the country to the local police chief. George's voice revealed his nervousness as he read. "The following missionaries are ordered by me to leave the country within twenty-four hours from the time this letter is received. The subversive actions of the named make them criminals of the state."

George then read the names of Barry and Virginia Vogle, Don and Ellen Hall and he and his wife, Ann. Barry, who was sixty miles from home, looked at his watch. "Maybe I can still make it home and back before dark. If I could only get word to Virginia, she could have things pretty well packed by the time I get there."

Barry went into the guest bedroom to get his suitcase. He shook hands with George and Ann and then hurried to his truck.

13

He decided to stop at a gas station in town instead of using what he had in the three jerry cans in the back of the truck. As he approached the river at the edge of the city, he was greatly concerned about the ferry he had to use. At times he had waited on the river bank for hours. But this time he was fortunate; the ferry was just leaving the opposite shore and there was no other truck in front of him. In an hour, the missionary was on the other side traveling full speed for the little bush station where he and Virginia had worked for a number of years.

As the distraught missionary pulled into the driveway, his wife came running from the house. "I've been packing, Barry. I heard the news of our expulsion on the radio." The words seemed too much for Virginia, and tears came to her eyes. "Why would the president do this to us, Barry? What have we done?"

"We haven't done anything, Honey, except preach the Word of God. If the Cultural Revolution conflicts with God's Word, then we must stand on the Word. That's why we're being expelled. The president wants to eliminate the opposition to his Cultural Revolution. One of the best ways to do it is to expel the missionaries."

It was difficult for the Vogles to know what to take with them on such short notice. They realized they were extremely limited, and it would be necessary to leave thousands of dollars of personal belongings and equipment which they had accumulated down through the years. Barry heard a truck outside and looked out just in time to see the local police chief drive in. He went out quickly to meet him.

"Hello, Mr. Renee. How are you?"

"I'm fine, Pastor Vogle, thank you. I have come to escort you people to the ferry. What is this all about anyway?"

"I really don't know, Mr. Renee, unless it's because God's Word, which I preach, conflicts with the president's Cultural Revolution."

The African official clicked his tongue. "You are correct, Pastor Vogle. I'm sure that's the problem. We must hurry, Pastor, because we're to meet another official at the ferry at six o'clock."

"But, Mr. Renee, it's almost that time now, and we haven't finished packing yet."

"I'm really sorry, Pastor Vogle, but you know I have to obey my orders. You people are such good friends, it grieves me very much to have to do this to you."

Within minutes, the veteran missionary couple walked out of their house, leaving behind many valuable belongings. The government truck followed several hundred yards behind as they traveled the sixty miles to the river. When they arrived, the ferry was already tied up for the night and the workers had returned to the village. On the opposite shore was another police officer who would take over the responsibility of the "criminals."

"They're sending a dugout canoe over for us," said Barry, pointing to the hollowed-log boat being paddled slowly across the river. With only minutes to work, he parked his truck under a tree and put his tool box, along with other valuables, in the cab, which he locked.

The Vogles shook hands with their police chief and stepped into the canoe. On the other side, there were more handshakes before they got into the cab of the police truck.

"They're taking us to the police station," Barry whispered to his wife. "I wonder where they have our co-workers."

As the missionary couple arrived at the city's police head-quarters, they were greeted with much commotion. "Follow me, Pastor and Mrs. Vogle," ordered the local police chief. "We have a room for you over here."

Barry recognized a number of Christian policemen whom he knew. Many of them waved and spoke as their missionary friends passed by. It was soon learned that the Winans and the Halls were also at the station but in separate rooms. A police secretary was brought in and wrote down extensive information about the missionaries. Around midnight, a guard walked into the dimly lighted room and announced that a truck was ready to take them on the 400-mile trip to the capital where they would board their plane for France the next day. Outside, they saw the other missionaries.

"How are we all going to fit into that Land Rover?" whispered Barry.

"I don't know," responded George. "I know it's going to be a tight squeeze."

The soldiers kindly but firmly ordered the missionaries into the small European pick-up. Virginia was told to ride in the cab with the chauffeur and the police chief. He was a Christian and was well-known to the Americans. Ann and Ellen stood directly behind the cab, and George, Barry and Don seated themselves on top of a gasoline barrel. The soldiers crowded in where they could find room. A number of them were Christians which made the missionaries feel a bit at ease with their rifle-toting guards.

The 400 mile trip through the night was an unbelievable ordeal for the six foreigners. The cold air chilled them to the bone. Their hands and faces became numb. It was a welcome sight when the light of the early morning sun made its way over the distant eastern horizon. After ten long hard hours of riding, they pulled up at the capital city's police station.

Barry was the first to jump down from the truck. To his surprise, he went sprawling face down in the dirt. He didn't realize he had no feeling in his feet and legs up to his knees. Even though they were in danger, the spread eagle dive of their co-worker brought a laugh from the other missionaries.

"You will stay here until your plane leaves this evening," said the capital's police chief. "I am a brother in Christ and will take good care of you. I hope there are no new orders from the president concerning you."

The officer then looked toward the restaurant several buildings down the street. "When you are hungry, let one of the guards know and he will see that you get something to eat."

"Sir," said George, "if we give you some money, would you buy us some mats and blankets so we can lie down to rest?"

Within a short time the police chief returned with the missionaries' purchases. As he handed the mats and blankets to the Americans, he asked again if they were hungry.

We haven't eaten in nearly twenty-four hours, Chief," said

Don. "We really would appreciate it if you could order something for us."

Within the hour, a Frenchman arrived with a large tray of food. After thanking the Lord for His provision and protection, Don looked up and smiled.

"This is a miracle," he said chewing on a piece of French bread. "Who would have ever thought that government 'criminals' would be treated like this?"

"And to have Christian guards, too," added Ellen.

The soldiers made things as comfortable as they could for the missionaries. No one was allowed to come and talk with them other than their guards. While they were resting on the mats, George nudged Barry and pointed with his chin to the main road. There stood a young man facing the Americans with an open brief case. Under the cover a sign was attached which read, "I am praying for you."

"It's marvelous the way the Lord has provided for us," said Don. "It has been difficult but, believe me, it could be a lot worse."

"You're right," responded George. "God has placed His people all along the way to care for us."

That afternoon the missionaries were taken to the airport and once again placed under heavy guard. The giant jet liner finally landed en route to France. The police chief with several others accompanied the prisoners to the plane. When they arrived at the steps, he stopped and stuck out his hand.

"Good-bye, my brothers and sisters. May God watch over you as you travel and take you safely back to your country."

The missionaries shook hands with their police escort and mounted the steps. At the top, Barry turned and waved to their African friends. A lump formed in his throat and his eyes filled with tears. The doors were soon closed, and the big airplane raced down the runway for takeoff. As it lifted from African soil, there were mixed feelings in the hearts of the six Americans. They were glad to be leaving Africa safely, but on the other hand, saddened to leave their precious spiritual fruit—their brothers and sisters in Christ.

2

RED LIKE CRIMSON

NINA KENDRICK

André, on wobbly legs, fighting waves of nausea, was the first one into the truck. Stumbling into a corner, he slumped to the floor, his head dropping onto his chest. A hot machine gun touched his hand. Wincing, he cursed silently. Relentless thoughts reeled through his head, keeping panic close to the surface.

I thought I was a tough soldier. . . . What would others think of me?

Laughing, shoving men climbed into the back of the truck. Pushing farther into the corner, André slouched lower. Usually he enjoyed the shady stories and rude songs that inevitably accompanied these trips. The truck motor sputtered, then roared into life, beginning the rough trip back to the barracks.

His best friend, Beta, called out, "Where is André? Did we leave him behind?"

André roused himself to respond. "I'm back in the corner." Using the tight quarters as an excuse, he once again closed his mind to all that went on around him.

Today was one day he was sure he would never forget. How could the awful scene ever be blotted from his memory? He would always see those pastors being mowed down by machine-

18

gun fire. Never would he forget the calm, quiet voices stating their choice to die rather than relinquish faith in their God. He shuddered at the remembrance of the bright carpet of crimson as they lay silent on the dusty ground. How proud André was that morning when he was chosen as one of the men for this special assignment. Seldom was one selected for a mission like this.

As the calm-faced "Jesus men" were packed into the truck, the soldiers hurled insults at them. André marveled that not one of them opened his mouth to respond to the taunts. His heart beat painfully with pity as he saw their wives and children huddled together in small groups, their faces masks of grief and fear.

Still, they had a job to do. To show pity was a sign of weakness. Quickly he rebuilt his armor of toughness.

Now that the terrible deed was accomplished, André discovered he really wasn't tough after all. He recalled how he had trembled when, at the order to shoot, he had pulled the trigger. He had never killed a man before. The sickness that welled up within him as he saw the men drop was something he never wanted to experience again.

"I can never forget . . . I can never forget. . . ." The words formed a chant in his head. He knew it was true. "I'll never forget those brave men whom I helped to murder." Yes, that was it, it *was* murder! He was a murderer!

André was surprised when the truck pulled in at the barracks. He hadn't been aware of the trip back. Usually the cramped space and lack of air under the heavy canvas gave him a headache. The bumpy road was always an annoyance, but today he had felt nothing.

Dazed, he crawled out over the tailgate. The men dispersed in all directions while the head man went to the office to make a full report.

In a desperate desire to cleanse himself from the evil of the day, André headed for the showers. No amount of scrubbing made him feel clean. Still damp and in a clean uniform, he headed out of town. His favorite pub was just minutes down the road.

Blaring music greeted him as he strode toward the tiny tavern enclosed in a lattice fence overgrown with bougainvillea vines. He was met at the entrance by Philomene, a girl in a tight dress.

"It's about time you came," she whined. "I've waited all day for you." Her mouth turned downward in an unbecoming pout.

André shoved past her and sat down at a small table sheltered by a couple of dusty potted plants. He was in no mood to listen to her nagging. But anything was better than sitting alone with his thoughts. He jumped up and, pulling her to him, he started to dance.

Philomene plied him with questions until, unable to tolerate her chatter any longer, he left her standing in the middle of the floor, mouth agape, as he stomped from the bar. Out in the dark, he turned away from the direction of the barracks and walked until his legs ached.

"What is wrong with me?" he grumbled aloud. "I must be turning soft. . . . I thought I was a good soldier!" His face flushed with shame and anger—shame for his weakness and anger for having run away. Turning abruptly, the young soldier headed back toward town.

He was amazed to feel warmth on his face as the sun in brilliant glory suddenly appeared. He had walked all night! No wonder his feet had begun to drag. He couldn't be late for roll call. In his agitation he had walked farther than he realized. His cousin Alphonse lived on this road. He would stop and borrow his bicycle.

As he neared the barracks on the rickety machine, his legs began to shake and rivulets of perspiration ran down under his hat. The horror of the day before returned in a flood, and the sickness came back to his stomach. What could he do to get rid of the pressing memories? Where could he go?

In the days following, André tried everything, filling every waking moment with frenzied activity. He danced, he walked, he talked endlessly with friends. When all else failed, he numbed his fevered brain with alcohol. Nights caused the most pain. Even when he fell into bed in a drunken stupor, the dream awaited him. The accusing eyes of the slain pastors followed him until he screamed in his sleep and awakened, shuddering and weak.

After several days André was close to exhaustion. One day his superior officer called for him. "Andre," he said, "there is something troubling you. Your work is inferior and you are nervous and irritable. Many have complained about your attitude. Are you ill?" Seeing the agony in the eyes of the youth, the officer finished kindly, "Can I help?"

"No sir, there is nothing wrong. I just haven't been sleeping well. It must be the heat." Outside under the hot sun, André was undecided about what to do. He had to get hold of himself, but how?

Not knowing why, he headed back to his bunk. He was grateful to find the big barnlike room empty. On his knees beside a brightly painted footlocker, he clawed frantically through his meager belongings. He drew out a small black Book. As his fingers slid over the smooth pages, he could hear his grandmother saying, "André, take this Book with you."

That was over a year ago, and the little volume had remained in the bottom of his trunk.

There were many underlined places on the thin pages. He flipped quickly through the Book as he muttered, "My head must be turning. Why am I looking at this old thing? My grandmother said it would help me but that is crazy." Words leaped from one page.

"Though your sins be as scarlet, they shall be as white as snow; though they be red like crimson, they shall be as wool" (Isa. 1:18).

"That's me, that's me!" André was soon outside running along the dirt road that led to his grandmother's village. It was over five miles but he was unaware of time or distance as he sped along, stumbling occasionally on the sharp stones. His only thought was to find out how he could be rid of the stains of sin that covered him. His grandmother knew; she would show him the way.

The rose and purple sky told him it was nearing sundown as he raced up to the mud hut of the white-haired woman. She sat by a diminutive fire, making her evening tea. He was astonished to see how unruffled the old lady was as she greeted him, almost as though she had been expecting him.

Words spilled out as he told her his story. The frail woman responded quiety, "Our pastor was one of those pastors. I'm sorry you had to be part of those dreadful killings. I prayed that God would send you to me."

Gently, she unfolded the wonderful story of salvation to her grandson. He was ready to lay down his burden of sin. And he was overwhelmed when he realized that Jesus was willing to save him, even though he was guilty of helping to murder some of His servants.

Later, the pastor's widow said to André, "Even though we miss him terribly, his death brought you to Jesus. I am very thankful; he would be too. He was old; you are young. Go now, my son, and live your life for the One Who gave His life for you."

As the young man left the village to hurry back to his work, he knew in his heart that that was exactly what he wanted to do. He wanted to spend the rest of his life telling everyone about his Savior.

3

THE SUITCASE MIRACLE

V. BEN KENDRICK

An ear-splitting crash of lightning sent Joan ducking down behind the front seat. She reached over and squeezed her husband's hand. "I'm afraid, Tim. I've never seen a storm like this before."

Tim and Joan Bilton were short-term missionaries who had arrived only three days earlier from America. They had come to New Guinea to work with Lee and Sandra Faber in their pioneer work. Lee sensed the uneasiness of the new arrivals and tried to cheer them.

"This is New Guinea," he said, keeping his eyes glued to the blurred windshield. "We can expect storms like this any time during the rainy season."

A loud noise from beneath the truck brought the pickup to a sudden halt. The vehicle leaned heavily to one side. Lee turned off the key and looked back at Tim and Joan. "As I was saying, this is New Guinea."

"What's wrong?" asked Sandra with a worried look.

"I don't know, Honey, but it sounded like either a mainspring leaf or a universal joint. As soon as the rain lets up, I'll see if I can get under the truck."

"How far are we from the mission station?" questioned Tim.

"About fifty miles," responded Lee. "On these roads, that's about four or five hours of travel."

In thirty minutes the rains slackened enough for the men to get out of the truck. Lee was surprised to find himself standing knee deep in water. Fortunately the back part of the truck was up out of the water. Lee was able to get his head under the pick-up just far enough to see the trouble.

"Just what I thought, Tim. The back universal is broken. There is no way for us to continue on with the truck the way it is."

"What do you plan to do?" asked Tim.

"There's a village about half a mile back. I'm going to get some men to push us out of the hole. Maybe we'll have to stay in the village until help comes . . . and that could be two or three days."

Within minutes Lee was sloshing through the mud on his way to the village. "Father, " he prayed, "please help us. I don't have an extra universal joint and I don't even know if there is one back in the capital city." Parts could be scarce at times.

The villagers knew Lee even though he didn't know them. They recognized all the vehicles in the area as well as their owners. As he entered the village, the first to meet him was the chief.

"Greetings, Mr. Faber. What brings you to my village, alone and all dirty?"

"My truck broke down, Chief. It's stuck in a hole just around that bend in the road." Lee pointed to the curve in the distance.

"You want my men to help you get out of the hole. Is that right, Mr. Faber?"

You are correct, Chief," answered the American. "I would like them to push me to a small clearing beside the road. The ground is higher there, and I'll be able to crawl under my truck."

"Do you have some sugar and salt with you?" asked the chief, smiling and showing his rotting teeth.

"Yes, we have both with us. We just did our shopping in the capital city."

"If my men push you out of the hole, you will give me some sugar and salt?"

"I'll be glad to give you some, Chief," responded Lee.

Without saying another word to the missionary, the tall scar-faced chief cupped his hand to his mouth and gave a loud command. Men immediately appeared from the little huts and made their way to their chief's side.

"Go with Mr. Faber. He needs help. Do as he tells you. Do not come back until he is through with you."

The chief then motioned for Lee to return to the truck. The men followed close behind.

A short time later, twenty-five strong men took hold of the pickup and literally lifted it out of the hole, pushing it to the clearing alongside the road. Tim stood shaking his head, amazed at their tremendous strength.

Lee lifted the canvas which covered the back of the truck. He found the case of sugar cubes as well as the bag of salt. The men lined up and he gave each one ten cubes of sugar and a handful of salt. Two small tins were filled and given to one of the men to take to his chief.

After the men left, the two couples went back into the cab to pray. "Lord," prayed Joan, "please do something for us. Somehow, Father, work a miracle for us and help us get to the mission station by tonight."

While Sandra was praying, Lee thought of a letter he had mailed to Tim and Joan three weeks earlier. He knew at the time that it would be a miracle for them to receive it before they left. Letters going to the states usually took at least a month . . . even air mail. When they finished praying, Lee looked excitedly at Tim.

"Did you get my last letter about the truck parts?"

Immediately Tim's face lit up. "Yes, we did. It came the day before we left."

Without another word, Tim got out of the cab and went around to the back of the truck. He lifted the canvas, pulled out a large brown suitcase and placed it on the hood of the pickup.

"Did you get the universal joints?" asked Lee, eagerly peering into the open suitcase.

Tim reached under some clothing and slowly pulled his hand out. There it was . . . a new universal joint!

"Praise the Lord," shouted Lee. "And to think it was there all the time."

We packed that one suitcase with things which we brought out for others," said Tim. "I forgot all about those parts you ordered. In fact, Joan and I were so busy getting ready to leave the next day that I simply gave the list to a friend of mine who owns a garage. He brought the box of parts over to the house that night and I packed them in this suitcase without even looking at them."

Within an hour Lee and Tim had jacked up the truck and put in the new universal joint. The rain had stopped and they made good time the rest of the way home.

That night as they sat around the dining room table, they recounted their experience of the day.

"I'll never forget this day," said Joan, smiling. "I asked God to get us here by tonight and to think," she giggled, "here we are. We had just the piece we needed in our suitcase all the time."

"You will have a good story to tell when you return home." said Lee.

"I sure will," responded Joan, "and when I do, I'm going to call it 'The Suitcase Miracle.' "

4

PATTY'S DOUBLE LIFE

V. BEN KENDRICK

Patty threw her book on the chair to show her disgust. "Oh, Mom! You're too narrow-minded. After all, Pete's not a criminal!"

"That will be enough of that, Patty," said Ann James, surprised at her daughter's outburst. "Why would you want to date an unsaved fellow anyway?" She hesitated a moment to get control of her voice. "You know, Honey, it would not be pleasing to the Lord."

"But, Mom," she responded, "Pete's the star baseball player. I'm sure any girl in school would love to go out with him. And besides, it would give me the chance to witness to him."

"Patty," spoke her mother, laying aside the dress she was hemming, "you know that violating one Christian principle will not help you keep another. Wrong is wrong, even if it is dating Pete Anderson so you can witness to him."

As she spoke, Patty's mother picked up a picture of her husband from the coffee table. He had been killed in a car accident two years earlier.

"Honey," spoke Ann James in a soft voice, "your father and I gave you to the Lord when you were born. Since you were a baby, we have prayed daily for you. I remember the night you accepted the Lord as your Savior. You were just eight years old.

Two years later you wanted to be a missionary nurse."

Patty looked at her father's picture. She remembered how she stood beside his casket and silently dedicated her life to the Lord for His service. Then something happened. She began going around with the wrong crowd at school. Before long she even became immune to their bad language. Right after Christmas vacation she met Pete. She was walking through the hall one day when he stopped her to ask her name. That led to other meetings and before long she was skipping classes to go with him to the nearby pizza house where many of the students hung out. At first, it was difficult for Patty to adjust to the loud music, but more and more she began to enjoy it. Her daily Bible reading and prayer times became something of the past. Sunday school and church became a bore. She attended only because she had to go along with her mother.

Patty saw the hurt in her mother's eyes. "Mom, please get with it. The world's not going to end simply because your daughter dates Pete Anderson."

Proverbs 22:6 flashed into Ann James' mind. "Train up a child in the way he should go: and when he is old, he will not depart from it."

"I don't want you to go out with him, Patty." As she placed the picture on the table, the burdened mother's eyes filled with tears. She took Patty into her arms. "Honey, I believe God has a life of fruitful service for you if you remain true to Him. Please don't do anything foolish. Patty, please listen to me. Commit this matter to the Lord. He'll help you."

"Mom, I can take care of myself very well. Pete's a nice guy. He doesn't even swear around me. You would really like him, Mom. I know you would."

That night Ann James prayed far into the night. "Lord, please speak to Patty's heart. Dear Father, bring her back into that sweet fellowship with Yourself."

The next day in school someone grabbed her by the arm. "Hey, Beautiful, what's your hurry?"

She turned to see Pete's smiling face looking at her. "Oh, hi, Pete." Her heart beat rapidly as she stood near him.

"Well, what's your answer, Patty?" he asked while stroking the top of her head. "Did your old lady give in or do we play it secret-like again and do a hide-and-seek game on her?"

Patty cringed at the way Pete talked about her mother, but brushed it aside thinking he meant well. "Mom says I can't go with you to the prom, Pete." She knew she could not tell him the truth, that she wasn't to date him at all. That would really end it for her.

"I hear your old lady's answer loud and clear, Baby, but I'm not taking her. I'm taking you, Beautiful. Now, what's YOUR answer?"

He put his arms around Patty and pulled her close. She looked to see if anyone was watching them. Feeling embarrassed, she stepped away.

"If I go to the prom, Mom will find out somehow, but if we go someplace where no one knows me, then there's no problem. I'll tell her my class is having a picnic. She'll believe that."

Patty couldn't believe her own words. She realized she was lying but she knew, too, she would lose Pete if she lived a Christian life. That night she told her mother she was going shopping with one of the girls from the church to buy her mother a birthday gift. Once she was out of sight from the house, she walked two blocks to the corner where she had arranged to meet Pete.

"Hi, Babe," he called as he pulled up to the curb, "hop in."

Patty opened the door and slid in beside the school hero. He immediately put his arm around her and sped away, leaving tire marks on the pavement.

"We're going to live it up tonight, Kid," Pete said. Patty noticed the slur in his speech. She realized Pete was drunk. He pulled her head over and kissed her. The smell of alcohol made her sick; fear gripped her heart.

"Pete," she said timidly, "I . . . I . . . I forgot to tell you. I can't stay out for more than an hour. I promised Mom I'd be right back."

"Listen, Baby," he laughed, "You and I are going to have a time tonight. We'll have some beers and then we'll take in that adult movie at the new drive-in. Your old lady's not going to see you until I'm good and ready to take you home. You hear me, don't you, Baby?"

"Lord," Patty prayed under her breath, "please help me." Never had she been so scared in all her life. It seemed as though a curtain had suddenly been lifted, and she saw the last several weeks flash before her.

"What a fool I've been," she said to herself. "Why? Why didn't I listen to Mom?"

Patty fought to keep back the tears. She couldn't believe she was actually riding in a car with her head on the shoulder of a drunken, unsaved man. The horror of it all overwhelmed her and she burst into tears. Pete pulled to the side of the road.

"Hey, what goes, Kid? You're not getting sick on me are you?" He opened the car door and stepped out.

"I've got to go home, Pete. I really do. Please believe me." As she spoke, the tears gushed from her eyes. "Pete," she sobbed, "I must tell you something. I'm a Christian. Christ is my Savior. I'm not the kind of girl you think I am. This fall, I'm going to Bible school to train to become a missionary nurse."

Pete stood as though in a trance as he listened to Patty.

"Since I met you, Pete, I've lived a double life. I live one life at home and church and another life at school and around you. That's wrong. I'm through living that way, Pete. I mean it. Please take me home."

Pete surprised her by turning the car around and heading back home. Patty sat beside the window in silence. Pete's face was set with anger. He pulled up to the curb. As soon as she closed the door, he pulled away with the tires squealing.

The short walk from the street to the front door seemed endless. Before Patty opened the door, the tears were flowing again. Within seconds she was inside and in her mother's arms.

"Oh, Mom! Mom!" she cried. "I'm sorry. I'm so sorry. Please forgive me."

Again Proverbs 22:6 flashed through the happy mother's mind. Her heavy burden was lifted. She knew Patty's double life was ended and she had her daughter back again.

30

5

TEAM WORK

V. BEN KENDRICK

Jim leaped high against the fence; he was just barely able to reach the ball, as he caught it in the webbing of his glove.

"Hey, Charlie, who's that new guy out there in left field?"

Tom White, the town mayor, stepped out of his parked car and made his way behind the batting cage where Coach Charlie Moore stood taking in the action on the field.

"Hello, Mayor White," said the serious-minded coach, "which guy are you talking about?"

The stocky mayor pointed to Jim as he raced to his right to backhand a sharp line drive.

"Why that's Jim Green," said Coach Moore. "He's a new student in school, trying out for that left field spot."

"He looks like a natural, Coach. How does he handle the bat?"

"Just like he fields that ball," grinned the proud baseball coach. "I'll have him hit a few for you, Mr. Mayor, if you aren't in a hurry."

"I'm going to knock you down with this one, Preacher," called the lanky fireball pitcher as Jim stepped to the plate.

"Hey, Preacher," yelled someone from the crowd of students standing nearby, "did you pray before you got in there with Lefty?"

Coach Moore looked at the Mayor and laughed. "The kid has religion and the guys like to get on him."

The tall redheaded pitcher wound up and threw a high, inside fastball forcing Jim to drop to the ground.

"Come on, Preacher," called someone else, "close your eyes and swing."

Jim got up and dusted off his uniform. He stepped back into the batter's box and smiled at Lefty who had fire in his eyes. The team's number one pitcher bent over and picked up the rosin bag. "I'll get you with this one, Green," he sneered. "You'll lose your religion on this pitch."

Jim knew that he faced a rough time with his teammates. He was new in town which only made his battle with the president of the senior class for the left field position more difficult. The players ridiculed him at every opportunity. They couldn't understand why he would not join their parties and do the same things they did.

Lefty double-pumped and let go with his best fastball. Jim's eyes were glued on the ball as it zoomed toward him with blazing speed. He swung hard, timing his swing perfectly. He knew he made solid contact. The center fielder never moved. The horsehide seemed to take wings as it headed for the center field fence. All eyes were on the ball as it cleared the fence at the 375 foot mark by thirty feet and landed in a field behind the ball park.

Mayor White shook his head. "I've seen a lot of hard hit balls but never anything like that drive. That kid's a hitter! That ball must have traveled 500 feet."

"He can do it, Mayor," said Coach Moore. "I don't care how much preaching he does around here as long as he keeps hitting like that."

Jim took several more swings sending three more balls out of the park.

"That's enough, gang," yelled Coach Moore. "Let's head for the showers."

"Hey there, Preacher," said Lefty as he came by Jim's locker, "you really hit me hard today. I'm glad you have that bat swinging for us."

"Thanks, Lefty," answered Jim with his familiar smile. "I'll be doing my best."

The tall left-hander moved closer to Jim. "Preacher, why don't you join us tonight? Some of us are taking in a new movie in town."

This was the first time the star pitcher had shown any friendliness to Jim since he started trying out for the team. Jim looked up at his teammate who was waiting for an answer. "Thanks for the invitation, Lefty. I really appreciate your asking me but you see, Lefty, I don't go to the movies. Besides, I always attend prayer meeting on Wednesday night." Jim hesitated. "Say, Lefty, why not come with me tonight? I'd love to have you meet some of my friends at church."

The tall pitcher looked like he'd been struck by lightning. "Church! Me go to church? You must be out of your mind, Preacher. Go peddle that stuff somewhere else."

At prayer meeting that night, Jim requested prayer for his teammates. In his heart he knew that Lefty would be his target as the Lord gave him opportunities to witness to him.

When Jim came to school the next day he sensed there was something wrong. He saw Coach Moore standing by the water cooler and hurried over to him. "Good morning, Coach. Did I hear something about an accident involving some kids here at school?"

"Yes, you did, Jim," answered Coach Moore. "Five of your teammates had a head-on collision late last night." The coach paused a moment to overcome his emotions. "Bud Mapes and Joe Spink were killed instantly. Lefty Williams, Sam Bender and Tom Rowe are in the hospital in serious condition. Lefty will never pitch again, Jim. He lost his right leg."

The news stunned Jim. "And to think," he said to himself, "that I was asked to join them." Jim moved down the hall to his first class. "Thank You, Lord," he prayed under his breath. "Thank You for saving me and giving me the privilege of living for You."

The next two days were sad days for the students at Wilson High School. A double funeral was planned for Saturday afternoon. Sam Bender and Tom Rowe showed remarkable improvement and were told by their doctors that they'd probably be discharged in a week or two. Lefty Williams was taken out of intensive care and informed he could begin having visitors on Sunday.

Jim was a bit nervous as he approached the hospital. "I wonder how he will receive me," he said to himself as he mounted the steps. "Lord, help me in this visit with Lefty."

"Hello, Lefty," said Jim quietly as he approached the still form on the hospital bed. "How are you feeling?"

Lefty tried to smile. "Hi, Preacher," he mumbled through puffed lips. "Glad to see you."

The next fifteen minutes passed by rapidly as the boys talked about the coming baseball season and the opening game the next afternoon. "I'll be rooting for you, Preacher. Hit one for me, will you?" A crooked smile spread across the young pitcher's face as his eyes filled with tears. The two boys shook hands and Jim promised he'd come back the next evening after the game.

Mixed emotions filled the student body on Monday at Wilson High. Every conversation seemed to be dominated by either the tragic accident or the opening game. With five members of the team missing, there seemed little hope of finishing anywhere but in last place.

Game time arrived with some 1,500 excited fans in the stands. Jim was surprised by Coach Moore's announcement right before the game, that he was named the team's captain. Throughout the early innings he couldn't help but think of his two dead teammates who had probably died without Christ. In his mind, he kept seeing Lefty in his hospital bed. The ninth inning began with Wilson High behind by two runs. The opposing team went down in order and then the home team had only three outs remaining. The first batter up in the bottom half of the ninth reached first base on a walk. The next man hit a line drive to the third baseman. With one out and one on, the next batter was nicked on the front of his uniform by the ball—putting runners on first and second.

34

Jim rose to his feet and headed for the plate. "Lord," he prayed, "help me to do my best for Your glory." As he stepped into the batter's box, he could hear Lefty's words, "Hit one for me, Preacher." Everyone was on their feet cheering for the new preacher-student. Jim took the first pitch high and inside. He swung on the next pitch and lined it foul down the left field line. Feeling a bit nervous, he stepped out of the box and rubbed some dirt on his hands. With the count at one ball and one strike, the tall team captain stepped back into the batter's box to await the next pitch. The little right-handed pitcher took his time on the mound. He took the sign, stretched and threw a burning fastball down the middle. Jim's eyes stayed with the ball until it made contact with the bat. It seemed as though he put every ounce of his 190 pounds into the swing. The ball took off like it was shot from a cannon. As Jim rounded third, the fans were already streaming onto the playing field. "We won, Preacher! We won!" someone shouted as they pounded Jim on the back.

The young Christian's heart was pounding with excitement as he walked down the hospital corridor. When he walked into the room, he was surprised to find Lefty sitting up in bed.

"You did it, Preacher! You won the game for Wilson." Lefty's face beamed as he spoke, "And just think, you hit a home run to do it."

Once again Jim saw tears in the redheaded boy's eyes. "Lefty," said Jim with a serious look on his face, "we can talk about baseball some other time. Right now, I'd like to tell you about my Savior."

"Go right ahead, Preacher. I'm ready to listen to you now."

Jim took a worn New Testament from his shirt pocket and turned to the Gospel of John. Lefty listened carefully as his friend read slowly from the third chapter and the sixteenth verse. "I see it, Preacher," said Lefty, wiping his eyes with his hand. "I see what He did for me. He died for me."

"That's right, Lefty. Jesus died for you and paid the penalty for your sins that you might believe and have eternal life."

A moment later, the red headed youth bowed his head, confessed his sins and accepted Christ as his Savior. There was a stillness in the room as the two finished praying. Lefty reached out and shook Jim's hand. "Thank you, Preacher. I feel like a new person."

"You are a new person, Lefty. You are now His child."

A grin spread across the swollen face. "Preacher, I want you to do something for me. I want you to tell Coach Moore and all the fellows that I'm inviting them to come to see me. I want them to come as soon as possible because I have something very important to tell each of them."

Jim patted his friend on the shoulder. "I sure will do that, Lefty. I'll call some of them tonight and tell the rest tomorrow."

Jim Green felt good as he left the hospital. He smiled to himself as he thought of "Preacher" Lefty and his desire to tell his teammates about Christ.

6

JUNGLE POTATOES

V. BEN KENDRICK

The small pickup truck left the sandy main road and started down a trail barely wide enough for it to pass between the trees.

"Thank you, Mr. White, for going this back road," said Goumba. "It will be so good to see my mother again after being away the past year."

Dan White and his African cook, Goumba, had been on the road for two weeks in an evangelistic outreach. They still had a day's travel ahead of them to reach home, but after hearing from Goumba that his unsaved mother lived only six miles off the main road, Dan felt led of the Lord to take an extra day and try to reach her village.

The going was slow, and there were several times when Dan thought they would surely get stuck in the deep mud which filled the many ruts along the path.

"It's right around the bend, Mr. White," said Dan's excited friend. "The villagers have already heard the motor and are gathering along the trail."

As the small bush village came into view, it was just as Goumba said. It seemed as if the whole village turned out to welcome them. Goumba sat straight up peering through the windshield hoping to catch a glimpse of his mother.

"There she is," he shouted, pointing to a little old woman who was sitting in front of a small round hut. "That's my mother, Mr. White."

As soon as the truck stopped, Goumba was out of the cab and running towards his surprised mother.

"Mama, Mama," he called. "It's me, Goumba. I've returned to see you."

The woman rose quickly from where she had been sitting beside a fire. "My son, I'm so happy to see you," she cried. Dan could see the tears running down her face as she greeted Goumba.

The next half hour was spent with Goumba visiting old friends and Dan making new ones. Everyone was filled with excitement over the new visitors.

"The chief says that we can sleep in that house over there Mr. White," said Goumba pointing with his chin at a nearby hut. Dan noticed that the chief had commanded several children to sweep out the hut and had a number of men unload the baggage from the truck.

"Mr. White," called the chief to Dan. "I'm glad you've come to visit my village. My people will do anything you ask of them to make you comfortable."

"Thank you, Chief," answered Dan. "We are happy to be with you."

Goumba appeared with his mother. "My mother wants to give you a gift, Mr. White."

The little woman then handed a small gourd to Dan.

"Thank you, Mama," said the young missionary as he looked into the gourd. "What are they?" he asked with a puzzled look on his face.

"They are jungle potatoes," answered Goumba, laughing. "They are very common in this area during the rainy season."

Dan could hardly believe his eyes. "Potatoes out here?" he said to himself. "Goumba, can we prepare them for our meal tonight?" he asked his African companion.

"We sure can, Mr. White," responded Goumba. "You see sir," he continued, "these jungle potatoes are very poisonous when they are dug out of the ground. They must be cooked, peeled and then soaked for three days in the stream. This gets the poison out of them."

Dan looked at the potatoes in the gourd.

"Don't be afraid to eat these potatoes," said Goumba. "There isn't any poison in them."

Dan turned to Goumba's mother, who stood beside him. "Thank you, Mama, for this wonderful gift. It has been many months since I last ate a potato."

The old African woman gave a big smile, showing her filed, pointed teeth. She then dropped to her knees in front of Dan, which was her tribal way of telling him that it was a privilege for her to give him such a gift.

That night as Dan fried the sliced potatoes over an open fire, he was thinking, "If Bev could see me now, she wouldn't believe that I am eating potatoes way out here in the bush." Even back at the mission station, Dan and Bev rarely had them to eat. They purchased their supplies sixty miles away in a small town. Only occasionally, on their monthly visits to the town, they would be fortunate to find potatoes which had been flown into their Central African country from France.

"These are delicious, Goumba," Dan said to his faithful friend, as they sat across from each other at their folding table.

Unknown to them, sitting off in the darkness, watching them eat their evening meal was Goumba's unsaved mother, who was thrilled to think that this visiting white man was so pleased to have her gift. When the last of the potatoes was gone, she quietly made her way through the tall grass to her hut with definite plans for the next day.

Goumba was busy building the fire for breakfast when Dan walked out of the hut, squinting his eyes from the bright sun just peeping over the distant hills.

"Good morning, Goumba. How are you this beautiful day?" Dan asked his traveling companion.

"I'm fine, thank you, Sir. Did you have a good night's rest?"

Before Dan could answer, Goumba added, "And how did those potatoes treat you?"

Dan laughed as he answered Goumba, "I had a very good night's rest, Goumba, and those potatoes sure hit the spot last night. Have you seen your mother, Goumba? I want to tell her how much I enjoyed them."

"I knew you would, Sir," said the African, blowing into the fire to get it started. "I've already sent for her; but they told me she has gone into the jungle and has left instructions for us not to leave until she returns."

Dan smiled as he heard what Goumba had to say. "That's all right with me, Goumba. We can remain here another day. That will give us opportunity to have another meeting with them tonight as well as give you another day with your mother."

Goumba looked at Dan. "Mr. White, pray that she will accept Christ before we leave. I can't bear the thought of leaving here knowing she is lost."

That morning and early afternoon, Dan and Goumba spent trekking out to the nearby garden villages to reach people who did not return to the main villages during the garden season. The two men visited garden after garden, and by early afternoon they headed back to their hut.

"Praise the Lord," Goumba said to Dan as they entered the village. "This has been a tiring day, but a very blessed one. I can still see that family of four as they received Christ as their Savior."

"And to think," interrupted Dan, "that they never heard the gospel before."

As they approached their hut, they were surprised to find Goumba's mother sitting on the ground in front of it. A huge basket was sitting beside her, filled to the top with potatoes.

"Hello, Mama," said Dan, reaching out for the usual handshake. "How are you today?"

She smiled, showing her pointed teeth. "I'm fine, my son. I brought you another gift that I want you to take home to your wife. It does my heart good to do this for you."

Goumba stood by listening with a big smile on his face.

"Thank you so very much, Mama," said Dan as he sat down beside her. "Thank you for this expression of your love for us."

40

He paused. "Mama, you've given me something. Now may I give you something in return?"

The elderly lady looked at Dan, nodding her head with approval.

Dan began to tell her about God's love for her and how He sent His Son to die for her so she could have forgiveness of her sins and have everlasting life. She sat quietly drinking in every word which was spoken to her.

"Have you ever asked Jesus to come into your heart, Mama?" he asked her.

With her eyes filled with tears, the old lady shook her head—"no." She was unable to speak.

"Would you like Jesus to become your Savior?" he then asked her.

She wiped away the tears from her eyes with her hands. "Yes, I would."

She looked up at Goumba. "I want the God Who has changed my son's life."

The villagers stood quietly by and listened. Goumba's eyes filled with tears as he stood praying for his mother.

"I do want Jesus as my Savior," she cried. "I want to know the God that you men love and serve."

Goumba knelt beside his mother.

In the diminishing light of the setting sun, the little old woman bowed her head and asked God to forgive her of her sins and to save her.

She then turned to Dan. "My son, you have been so good to me. You not only brought my son to see me but you gladly received my gift. Because you did this for me, I was willing to listen to you. Thank you for those good words about Jesus."

As Dan and Goumba started for home the following morning, Dan knew that when the dry season came he would be returning with Beverly to meet Goumba's mother who had given them their first jungle potatoes.

7

NOT FOR THE BIRDS!

NINA KENDRICK

The narrow edge of the sun rising on the horizon sent bright spears of light upward into the pale sky. The shimmering rays found entrance between the sunbaked bricks where the mortar had worn away and through the bare patches on the thatched roof of Esther's hut.

One tiny beam with its warm finger touched Esther's quiet, brown face as she lay sleeping deeply.

In one motion, her eyelids flew open and she was on her feet, wrapping the threadbare cloth around her thin frame and tucking the ends in at her waist.

Fretfully she roused the children and sent one scurrying for peanuts from the giant storage basket in back of the hut. The peanuts were for planting as soon as they got to the garden. They were late this morning. Normally, Esther would have been up long before the sun had first peeped over the distant hills.

"How could I have slept so late?" she grumbled, more to herself than to the girls.

Quickly she prepared food for her little family. The breakfast of manioc bread and hot, bitter coffee was soon eaten. They all realized there was much work to be done that day, and there would not be time to eat a large noonday meal. With their hunger satisfied, all four hurried along the rough, narrow path that led to the clearing which was their patch of garden. The two older girls matched the tempo of their flying feet to that of a song they had learned in children's class a week ago.

> Nzapa ndoye sesse so, sesse so,
> sesse so, Nzapa ndoye sesse so, Lo
> ndoye so minqui.

The song, which tells of God's love for the whole world, is sung to the tune of "Mary Had a Little Lamb." It made good accompaniment for the little feet as they raced along, prodded from behind by Mama.

The rapid pace of mother and daughters stirred up excitement along the path. Now and then a rabbit would be startled from its rest or a partridge sent fluttering just above the top of the grass. Once the girls screamed with fright and stopped in their tracks as a huge warthog scurried across the path only a few yards in front of them!

Sarai, the little one, stubbed her toe on a hump of dirt the ants had raised in the path during the night. Esther jerked her to her feet and hurried her along. Nothing else must delay them this morning. They must get the peanuts into the ground today. The bank of clouds piling up beyond the hills told Esther that it would rain before evening. The ground was just right for planting after yesterday's shower, and today's rain would give them just the start they needed. Most of her neighbors already had their gardens sown.

Finally they entered the last thicket of brush and trees before coming to the garden. The narrow path gave the appearance of a tunnel through the undergrowth. In minutes, they burst out into the bright sunshine of the little clearing which was their garden.

The largest share of the little plot of ground had already been cleared. It was not an easy task—pulling weeds, digging out partially burned stumps, breaking up the hard packed clumps of earth and smoothing out the furrows. All this was done with the use of handmade hoes.

By the time the blazing sun was directly overhead, the red-brown soil was ready for planting. Sarai was whimpering softly now; she was tired and hungry. Esther's mahogany features glistened with wetness. She too was aching with fatigue. Calling the other girls from their work, she untied the small bundle she had brought with her. A chunk of dried meat and a piece of bread was handed to each child. Eagerly they ate the food, and washed it down with tepid water from a highly polished gourd.

"Mama, that was so good," whispered little Sarai who was already stretched out in the cool shade. She had bundled some grass and leaves together to make a small pillow. "Can we have just a little rest?" she continued. "I am sure that Ruth and Lois are thinking the same thing, Mama."

Esther could not help smiling, but knowing there was still much work to do, she stood to her feet and called the older girls to her. Carefully she divided the peanuts among them and with concise instructions, admonished them to plant just as she had told them.

"We can easily get the seeds all planted by the time the day dies if you work as I have told you," Esther called to the girls as they bent to the task with something less than enthusiasm.

The children had already worked very hard and they were tired, but they knew Mama meant what she said. She expected the seeds to be planted by evening, and what Mama wanted, she usually got! Besides, the girls knew what this peanut crop would mean to them. Not only would the peanuts provide nourishing food, but if they had a good crop they would sell the excess and have money for much needed clothing.

With these thoughts in mind, every member of the family doubled their efforts to get the job done; even Sarai did her share of the work.

As the afternoon wore on, they were sure they would be successful. Surely they would get the planting completed today. A feeling of exhilaration partially erased the weariness of their sore bodies. By the time the sun was a fiery, red-orange ball and appeared to be about a yard's length from the faraway hills, the last peanut had been carefully placed in the last hole. Clutching her back, Esther slowly straightened and heaved a tremulous sigh of relief. It was finished, with at least an hour to spare before dark!

"Thank You, dear Father, for helping us." she prayed.

Raising her eyes toward Heaven in a gesture of thankfulness, Esther gasped. That very black cloud swooping down toward them wasn't a rain cloud. No, it was birds! And how those birds loved peanuts! In a matter of minutes, they would clean out their hours of hard work! Worst of all, if these peanuts were taken, there were no more. Sarai had scooped out the very last handful that morning. They had no money to buy more. What would happen to them if they lost their precious peanut crop?

With a prayer to her Heavenly Father, she ran to the center of the clearning. While the three children watched their mother in astonishment, Esther shook her fist at the birds and shouted, "You keep right on going. God knows how much we need these peanuts. He won't let you eat the seeds. Go away and find your food somewhere else!"

A miracle took place. In spite of the attractive, freshly dug and freshly planted garden, the flock of birds flew right on by, leaving the peanut garden untouched. The little family jumped and shouted for joy at what had happened. Even Esther could not keep from showing her excitement as she clapped her hands and shouted, "Thank You, Lord! Thank You, Lord!"

While the weary little family trudged back along the jungle path heading toward home, sixteen-year-old Lois turned to look into her mother's careworn face.

"Mama," she said, "you have always told us how God takes care of our needs. I always believed it, Mama, because you said it. But Mama, today God *showed* us how He cares for us. Today He gave us a picture lesson I will never forget. Why, Mama, He made those birds listen to you!"

A crystal drop rolled out of Esther's eye and slid down her cheek, landing on top of tiny Sarai's curly head. A smile trembled on her lips as she replied, "Yes, Lois, God did make those birds listen, and our garden this year will be a fine testimony of His love and His care for those who trust Him."

Later that week, amid some chuckles and a few tears, Esther gave her testimony in the midweek prayer meeting. Everyone in the village knew and loved Esther and rejoiced when she rejoiced. The group of believers listened attentively as she recounted the garden experience. Her closing words were from Psalm 37:3, "Trust in the LORD, and do good; so shalt thou dwell in the land, and verily thou shalt be fed."

Esther had trusted in the Lord. He had caused the birds to fly right over her garden, and she knew her family would be fed. They would have a fine crop this year. Hadn't she seen the tiny green sprouts already pushing up through the earth today? Once again God had taken care of His faithful servant, and once again she was able to share with her friends the evidence of His loving care.

8

ED'S CHOICE

V. BEN KENDRICK

The loud thump against the side of the building caused Jim to look up from his books and glance at his watch. "What could that be at this time of night?" the missionary camp director asked himself, stepping from the camp office into the darkness. "It's eleven o'clock."

A sickening thud followed by a groan turned Jim's attention to the direction from which the sounds had come. Someone was standing motionless in the shadows, and a form lay on the ground nearby. The missionary pulled his flashlight from his hip pocket. There in the bright beam was Ed Jones, one of the new campers. On the ground before him was another camper, Mike Best—his face covered with blood.

"Ed!" called Jim, racing toward him. "What's going on here?"

Without saying a word, the camper pulled a switchblade from his pocket and leveled the point toward the missionary's stomach. "One more step, Mr. Lane, and I will kill you."

The camp director saw the serious glint in the young man's eyes. "I'm not going to fight you, Ed. Just hand me the knife and let's talk this over."

Jim stepped boldly to within two feet of the shining steel. He reached out and slowly took the knife from the Indian. Dropping to his knees, Jim examined Mike's cut face. Mike regained consciousness and was taken to the nurse's cabin for treatment.

News of what had happened spread like wildfire. The next morning the whole camp knew that Ed Jones had pulled a knife on the camp director. After breakfast the staff met for their daily meeting.

"I think you should send him home, Jim," said one of the other men. "It's not safe for him to be around the other campers. He's just plain wild."

"I understand what you are saying," responded Jim, "but I see something good in that boy. I just can't send him home."

The rest of the week passed with only minor incidents involving Ed. He was a bit noisy in the class sessions, but that was to be expected from one who was known for his rough ways back on the reservation. No one near his age or size tangled with him in his home territory. His knife and fearlessness had earned him a bad reputation throughout the reserve.

Ed sat in the front seat with Jim as they traveled back home. The missionary smiled at his young friend as he spoke. "It was great to have you at camp, Ed. When we get back to the reservation, I'll give you your knife."

"I would have killed anyone else, Mr. Lane, for doing what you did that night. For some reason I just could not hurt you."

A deep mutual friendship began developing between the two during the next few days. The day before Jim was to return to camp for another week, he received a surprise visit from Ed.

"I hear you are going back to camp, Mr. Lane." As Ed spoke, Jim noticed the switchblade sticking out of his hip pocket. "Can I go back with you?"

The camp director looked hard at his Indian friend. Again, he sensed the great potential of the boy before him. "You can go on one condition, Ed. You can't take your knife. I don't want you to get into any trouble at camp."

"You have a deal, Mr. Lane," spoke the Indian, handing his knife over to the missionary. "When do we leave?"

Early the next day Jim Lane drove out of his driveway with

Ed Jones beside him. The young man seemed somewhat subdued as they made their way through the reservation to the main highway.

"What do I do, Mr. Lane, if one of the other guys pulls a knife on me? I can't even defend myself."

"Don't worry about that, Ed," answered the missionary. "Switchblades aren't allowed at camp and besides nearly all the kids are Christians."

Ed sat in silence as he thought about the director's response. Deep down in his heart was a yearning to have what the missionaries and some of the campers had. He was too proud, however, to admit such a need to anyone—even the camp director.

During the third day of camp it happened. Jim had just finished teaching the campers a new song and then asked for testimonies. One after another stood to his feet to tell what Christ meant to him. Ed sat listening to every word. He knew his heart was not right before God, and beads of perspiration stood out on his face. Suddenly he stood to his feet. Silence swept over the room and Jim Lane smiled. Ed's lips moved slightly without a sound. Finally he spoke.

"I am different than most of you in this room. You speak of knowing Jesus and what He means to you. I . . . I . . . I can't do that. You see, I do not know Him like you do."

Most of the kids bowed their heads as Ed spoke. Some were praying for him. Jim Lane continued to smile as he listened to the boy from his reservation.

"I want to have Jesus as my Savior, Mr. Lane," continued Ed. "Up to this time, I refused to even talk to you about Him, but I can't go on feeling the way I do. My heart is very sinful. I need help from your God, Mr. Lane, I really do."

Within minutes Ed publicly prayed and asked God to forgive him of his sins and to save him. As soon as class was over, the campers swarmed around the new Christian.

The rest of the week was different for Ed Jones. His attitude changed completely. Kids who had sidestepped him before, went out of their way to talk with him. The last day of camp, Ed asked permission to speak at the noon meal. He was nervous as he stood looking over the group of campers.

"I owe most of you an apology. I have fought with some of you, called many of you bad names and stolen from nearly all of you. I ask your forgiveness before I return home to my people." Ed hesitated and then spoke again. "I ask you to pray for me. I live with my father and have two brothers and two sisters. None of them know Jesus as their Savior."

That evening, Jim and Ed arrived back on the reservation. The missionary dropped his Indian friend off at his father's house and then continued on home where Evelyn had supper on the stove waiting for him. Little did he realize that as they ate their meal, Ed lay unconscious on the floor of his father's house with blood streaming from a deep gash in his scalp. His father and brothers stood nearby, and one of them clutched an iron pipe. Ed had just told them about his faith in Jesus.

Evelyn Lane looked out the kitchen window just in time to see a blood-spattered head pass by. She quickly put down the dish she was drying and ran to the door.

"Jim! Come quickly! Someone's hurt!"

Evelyn's legs weakened at the sight which met her as she opened the door. She found herself staring into the battered face of Ed Jones, the new Christian. "Ed! What happened?"

Slowly the teenage lad spoke through puffed lips. "My father and brothers beat me up, Mrs. Lane."

"But . . . but, why? What did you do to them?"

"I accepted Jesus as my Savior, I defied my father's gods."

Within minutes Jim and Evelyn were busy washing and putting medicine on Ed's wounds. The cut from an iron pipe was the most severe.

"I'll take you to the hospital to get some stitches in that one," said Jim. "It's cut right to the bone."

Things were rather quiet around Ed's home for the next week. He told the missionaries he was only tolerated by his family. A great deal of his time was spent on the mission station where he helped in any way he could. Several times his father and brothers threatened to beat him but somehow he always

50

managed to escape. The young Indian attended church faith-fully. At first his only clothing consisted of a pair of jeans and a T-shirt, but Jim and Evelyn helped him get other clothing. Two times that winter Ed received terrible beatings at the hands of his father and brothers, but that did not stop his attendance at church or deter his desire to live for Christ.

Near the end of May, Ed Jones was baptized and joined the church. Standing off in the distance under some trees were his father and brothers, determined more than ever to seek revenge for his defying their tribal gods.

That night Jim saw someone stagger into the mission com-pound. At first he thought it was Ed, but then dismissed that thought from his mind since the man he saw was obviously drunk. He stepped out the side door to meet the visitor.

"Hello, uh . . . uh . . . , Mr. Lane," came a greeting in slurred speech.

"Ed Jones! What has happened to you?"

The Indian's clothing was soaked with beer. The smell of it permeated the air.

"They made me drink it, Mr. Lane. The poured it all over me and forced me to swallow it."

Even though he was drunk, Ed knew where to go for help and what he wanted to tell his missionary friends. "It's not my fault, Mr. Lane. Will God forgive me? Will He, Mr. Lane?"

Jim took Ed to the garage where he helped him get cleaned up and into some clean clothes. In the meantime, Evelyn made some strong coffee for their Indian friend. Within an hour, Ed was much better. Jim invited him to stay at the mission station for the night. He knew that Ed's father and brothers were determined to harm him.

A week later, Jim and Ed went to camp. This time Ed was part of the staff.

"It does not seem possible, Mr. Lane," said the smiling Indian, "that I am really going to be able to work at camp all summer."

"It will be nice to have you, Ed." responded the camp director. "God has done some wonderful things for you."

Because of his background, Ed was able to communicate well with the other Indians who were having the same problems he experienced. The summer proved to be an outstanding camp season. Ed's popularity among the Christian young people grew as he became the secret hero of many. The last day of camp was an unwelcome one for Ed who knew that much persecution awaited him back on the reservation.

"Good-bye, Ed," called Mike Best. "It was great to be here with you this week."

A sad feeling swept over Ed as he thought of the time he beat up on Mike. How thankful he was for his new life in Christ. He and Mike had grown to be very close friends.

The trip back to the reservation seemed to pass quickly for Ed as he and Jim talked over the events of the camp season.

"I've been praying for your father and brothers and sisters, Ed. My heart has been greatly burdened for them."

"Thank you, Mr. Lane. If they get saved, it will take a great miracle. My father and brothers are very wicked men and would even murder to get what they want."

The two friends arrived just as the sun began to dip behind the distant hills. Jim noticed someone standing in the shadows of nearby trees as he dropped Ed off at his father's house. The missionary felt uneasy regarding the safety of his friend, but as an outsider there was nothing he could do.

As Jim pulled into the drive he saw Evelyn sitting on the porch. "I'm really burdened for Ed, Evelyn," he said, approaching the front steps. "I had a strange feeling about leaving him today. I'm sure the Indian grapevine has brought back reports of his good ministry this summer."

The missionary couple spoke about a number of things during their meal, but each conversation returned to the topic of their Indian friend, Ed Jones.

Jim opened his eyes and listened. Was he dreaming or did he really hear someone knock? There, he heard it again. Someone was knocking on the front door. He jumped out of bed and pulled on his robe.

"What is it, Jim?" asked Evelyn, sitting up in bed.

"Someone's at the front door. I wonder who it could be at three o'clock in the morning?"

Jim glanced out the window and recognized the police uniforms and quickly opened the door.

"Sorry to bother you this time of night, Rev. Lane, but we are making an investigation on a suicide."

"A suicide!" repeated the missionary. "Who is it?"

The police officer was serious as he spoke. "Ed Jones, Sir. He committed suicide about an hour ago. He shot himself in the heart."

"Ed Jones!" cried Jim. "I just dropped him off at his father's house last evening."

"I'm sorry, Rev. Lane, but it's true. Ed Jones is dead."

The funeral was a very sad one for the Christian community. People came from far and near to pay their respects to a fellow believer. Ed's father and brothers talked and laughed throughout the service. It was difficult for Jim to understand their actions. When the service was over, the father and his sons retreated to their cars where they promptly began drinking beer.

Three weeks after the funeral, Jim was in town buying some supplies. As he was leaving the small general store, he passed one of Ed's brothers.

"Hello, Tom," said the missionary. "How are you? I haven't seen you since your brother's funeral."

"Hello, Mr. Lane," responded the young Indian man. "I want to talk with you about something that is bothering me."

The two men made their way outside to a secluded area under some trees. Tom was nervous as he spoke.

"What I am going to tell you, Mr. Lane, is true. I did not do it, but I know the one who did."

"What are you talking about, Tom?"

"About Ed's death, Mr. Lane. I heard you questioned the suicide note at the police station and you were right in doing that. One of my brothers printed that note."

"But, what about the shooting, Tom? Who did that?"

"I can not tell you, Mr. Lane, but it was done by one of our family. When Ed came home that night, we overpowered him when he came into the house. We thought of beating him to death, but we knew we would get in trouble with the law for doing that. Then we decided the best thing to do was to write a suicide note and shoot Ed."

"Did Ed say anything before he died?"

"Yes, he did. We told him he could live if he would deny Jesus and come back to our father's gods. He told us that he would never deny his Savior. In fact, he told us that God loved us and Jesus could become our Savior, too, if we would accept Him."

Tom stopped talking and for a moment stared off into the distance. He then continued with his story.

"We became so angry with him, my father wanted to finish him off with a knife. We persuaded him the gun would be better and that was it. The sound was muffled and Ed was dead. Mr. Lane, my brother chose to die for his faith."

Author's Note: In order to protect the people and the work involved, the names in this story were changed and no locations were mentioned. To indicate the seriousness of the situation, one of Ed's sisters approached the missionary at a later time and told him she wanted to accept Jesus as her Savior, but if she did, it would mean certain death for her.

9

THE WINDOW

NINA KENDRICK

"Ohhhh. . . . it's so beautiful!" Susan Wainright sat straight in her wheelchair and gazed upward at the stained glass window high above the pulpit in the little church. The tiny child in a dress of primrose yellow, her shiny golden hair falling in soft waves around a strikingly beautiful oval face, tightly clasped the hand of her mother, Emily.

"Mommy, it's so beautiful," she repeated in a whisper.

Emily Wainright smiled at her daughter as tears slid down her cheeks and squeezed the soft little hand in response.

This was a very special day for the Wainrights. It represented four long years of sacrifice for Emily, Susan and the two boys, Jeff and Craig. Each of them recalled that terrible day when their strong, handsome daddy and husband had been taken from them. A single blow on the head by a fleeing burglar had halted the vibrant life of the young patrolman, leaving a dazed and desolate family behind. Even little Susan, who had been scarcely three at the time, vividly remembered that dreary, drizzly day and the early morning visit of her father's chief.

When the funeral was over, Emily began the task of picking up the pieces of four shattered lives. Phil's insurance would take care of most of the big things, but she knew immediately that she would have to go to work. The boys were in school and well provided for, but what about Susan? The baby girl they had longed for had been born with a spinal defect, and they knew from the beginning that she probably would never walk. But what joy she had brought to them! Her sunny disposition, in spite of the handicap, had made her everyone's favorite.

When Ellen Flagg, the neighbor two doors down the street, had offered to keep Susan while Emily worked, she protested such kindness.

"Nonsense! With my own six rowdies," Ellen laughed, "we won't even know there is another child in the house!"

There remained a nagging doubt. The Flaggs were not Christians. Could she leave her precious baby with people like that? But Susan, even at such a tender age, loved the Lord Jesus. By the end of the second week there were six Flagg children in Sunday school. It took a little longer for Bill and Ellen, but with quiet encouragement from Emily and more vigorous pleading from Susan and six little Flaggs, soon an entire pew near the front was occupied by their family.

In a family conference one day, Jeff and Craig declared it was time they had a memorial for their father. He had been respected and loved in their small town. Everyone knew his Christian stand and many had been won to the Lord through his testimony.

"What sort of memorial did you have in mind, boys?"

"I'm not sure, Mom," Craig spoke first. Then looking lovingly at his sister he continued, "Susie, maybe you have an idea."

Pansy blue eyes sparkled as Susan clapped her hands and squealed. "I know, I know . . . a stained glass window, a beautiful stained glass window. Our daddy loved pretty things. He would love a stained glass window!"

Tears filled her eyes and the eagerness died on her face when silence deep and long followed her suggestion.

"You don't like my idea," she said over a sob.

Three sets of arms reached to embrace the little girl.

"We love your idea, Susie. It is the most beautiful of ideas, and you are right. Daddy would love a stained glass window. We

56

were just overwhelmed at such a lovely thought. Thank you, Honey, for being such a wise little girl!" Emily exclaimed.

"It will take a lot of money so we'll have to give up some things. It will take some time, but we'll do it!"

"Hooray for Susan," shouted the boys.

It did take some time . . . four years. They gave up a lot of life's simple pleasures and spent a long time hunting for someone to do the job, and they were finally able to have the exact kind of window they wanted. The red glass had to be imported, so it was very expensive, but their window had to have lots of red glass. Red was Phil's favorite color. He had always said it reminded him of the blood of Jesus, his very dearest Friend.

No one complained of any lack. They all looked forward to the day when their dream would become a reality. That day finally arrived. People from all over town came to pay tribute to the memory of their friend Phil, the policeman.

The dedication was just as they had requested. The plan of salvation was clearly outlined for their friends who did not know the Lord Jesus. Several were saved, and others were drawn closer to the Savior they already knew and loved.

Emily, her heart aglow, felt peace and contentment as she pushed the wheelchair toward home. The children chattered excitedly about the events of the day.

Week after week the congregation enjoyed the glorious colors of the window. On sunny days it cast a vivid rainbow over the communion table beneath the pulpit.

One warm spring day, as the Wainrights approached the church, people stood about in small circles talking quietly. Emily couldn't understand why everyone turned to look at them without their usual cheery greetings.

"I wonder what is going on," she mused as they entered the building. Just then she heard Susan gasp.

"Mommy. . . . the window. . . ." She sat staring at the place where an ugly piece of gray plastic was taped to the gaping hole.

Hurrying toward them, the pastor held out his hand. "I'm so sorry you had to learn it this way. I tried to call you, but you must have left home a littler earlier than usual. The window was stolen last night!" He patted Susan's head and went on.

"There was nothing to indicate how it was taken. I left here about six o'clock last evening and saw no one loitering around the building. Stained glass windows bring a great deal of money. I'm so sorry, Emily, children. Only a miracle will bring it back."

Everyone was too stunned to take part in a regular service that morning. Pastor Dorvan led the congregation in prayer.

"Dear Jesus," prayed Susan, in a tear-drenched voice, "please make whoever took our window bring it back."

Weeks passed and still the ugly hole remained in the church wall. The police found nothing to lead them to the thief. Meanwhile, Emily watched Susan with concern. The doctors had long ago warned that the little girl would probably not reach adulthood. When Phil had died, she found such comfort in her daughter that the thought was thrust far back in her mind. Now, however, she realized that all was not well. She made an appointment at the city hospital where they were familiar with Susan's case. She hoped it was just the missing window that was upsetting Susan.

Instead of driving the thirty miles, Emily decided to take the train. A friend drove them to the drab little station, and aided by a friendly conductor, Jeff gently lifted the child from her wheel chair, carried her to her seat and placed the folded chair nearby. After promising his help at the end of the line, the conductor went about his duties, and Jeff bade them farewell.

Mother and daughter were quiet for awhile, as they enjoyed the ever-changing view, but suddenly Susan turned to Emily with tears coursing down her pale cheeks. "That church we passed, Mommy, did you see it?" she choked. "The beautiful window reminded me of our window. If only we could find it!" The sentence ended in a wail, and people on every side turned to look at the weeping child. Tongues clucked in sympathy while the people wondered why a window caused such turmoil.

The doctors confirmed Emily's worst fears. The deterioration was progressing rapidly now, and they could offer little hope. Seeing her mother's despair, Susan whispered, "Don't

58

worry, Mommy, when Jesus takes me I'll be with Daddy. And I won't have to be in a wheelchair any longer either."

From that day it seemed they could actually see Susan slipping away from them. The family and their friends all helped to make her days especially happy, even though their hearts bled. But the window—if only the window could be restored!

Early one morning the pastor phoned the Wainright home. "Emily," he said, "is Susan well enough to come by the church for a few minutes?"

It was late October, but still sunny and warm. . . . a beautiful Indian summer day. Without asking the reason, Emily replied, "She slept well last night. A walk in this beautiful weather will do us both good!"

Bright sunlight flooded the church while brilliant colors shimmered across the carpet. The window was in place!

Speechless, Susan sat drinking in the beauty while Emily turned to Pastor Dorvan with a questioning look on her face. Without speaking, he handed her a soiled piece of paper, and her eyes filled with tears as she read the words:

"We couldn't let the little gurl with the angel face be sad no more. We was on the trane and saw her cry on acount of a church winda. We figure it was the one we was takin to the city to sell. . . ."

"It was on the church steps last Wednesday morning. I waited until after we got it back in place to tell you."

"Thank you," Emily whispered, sinking into a chair next to Susan. "God really *did* perform a miracle."

Jewel-like hues flickered across the small white casket. Susan was enjoying Heaven now with her daddy. The window would serve as a memorial to both of them, but more important, it would always be a symbol of their love for their Savior, the Lord Jesus, who had shed His blood for them, and with Whom they were now sharing a home in Heaven.

10

THOSE LAST WORDS

V. BEN KENDRICK

Phil Smith laid the letter on the table and stared out the window.

"What is it, Phil?" asked his mother who stood nearby. "Is it bad news?"

The tall, Bible-college student picked up the letter from the table and handed it to his mother. "It's from the business office. I'm told that I won't be able to return to school this fall because of my debt. I still owe them $900, and I don't see how I can earn that much more in the jobs that I have this summer."

Ann Smith looked at her son with an encouraging smile. "We wish we could help you, Phil, but you know that your father's recent medical expenses have taken practically all our savings, and with Dad not able to work yet, we must watch every cent we spend."

Phil saw the hurt in his mother's eyes and realized again how much she wanted him to continue his schooling that fall. He had already applied to the mission board and planned to appear before the council for his oral examination, and he had also planned to attend the candidate seminar immediately following his graduation. Ever since Phil dedicated his life to the Lord for missions at the age of ten, his parents had been his chief source of encouragement and had helped him as much as possible.

In his first year of college, during the annual missionary conference, the Lord had laid the needs of Haiti upon Phil's heart. Missions seemed to become the very heartbeat of Phil's life. The day in his junior year the candidate secretary for a mission board visited the college was a day which Phil would long remember. His face lit up with excitement as the mission official explained the candidate procedures to him.

"You can apply now, Phil, if you believe God has called you to be a missionary," said the tall, pleasant-looking man. "You really don't have to wait until you graduate to apply. In fact," he went on, "we encourage application to the mission when one is completing his junior year and ready to begin his last year of school. That way, you can complete all your necessary paper work and appear before the mission board shortly after graduation as well as attend our candidate seminar in July."

That night Phil had called his parents to tell them the good news. "That's right, Dad," he said excitedly, "I have my preliminary application here in my hand as I talk with you. It's hard to believe I'm finally applying to serve the Lord in Haiti."

If Phil could have seen his father on the other end of the line, he would have seen that beloved face streaked with tears of joy. Sam Smith bowed his head as he placed the receiver in its cradle.

"Lord," he prayed, "I ask You to direct our Phil and meet his every need." Sam, like his wife, Ann, was thrilled that their only child was going to be a missionary.

Now, some months later as they sat across from each other at the table, Ann and Phil stared at the letter.

"The Lord sent you to Bible college, Phil, and He'll supply your needs somehow. Whatever way He chooses will be the very best way. We can be sure of that."

That night after Phill got home from work, he was reading his Bible before going to bed. The verse seemed to jump out of the pages at him. "Faithful is He that calleth you, who also will do it" (1 Thess. 5:24).

Phil slipped down on his knees beside his bed. "Thank you, dear Father," he prayed. "Thank You for assuring me that You will supply my needs as I follow Your leading."

The summer seemed to pass quickly. Phil's father made a good recovery and was able to go back to work. Phil worked hard in his two jobs. The one at the furniture store was the better paying job, but since he needed the money and Mr. Jones needed help, he took on the three hours at the gas station each night. To add to Phil's financial burden, another letter came from the college, informing him that there would be an increase in tuition in the fall. This, combined with his present debt, made the situation nearly impossible for him.

It was almost closing time at the station one evening, in the middle of August, when an unexpected phone call came. "Phil, it's Mom. Oh, Phil," she began to cry softly, "It's Dad. I think it's his heart. Come home quickly."

Phil's own heart skipped a beat as a cold chill ran through him. "Did you call the doctor, Mom?"

"Yes, and he's sending an ambulance right over. The doctor is on his way here, too."

"I'll be right home, Mom. I should be there in a few minutes."

Phil arrived just as Dr. Stanton entered the house. He had never seen his father so sick. The gray look on Sam's face and the difficulty he had breathing indicated his serious condition. The ambulance arrived and in minutes, was on its way to the hospital with its precious occupant. Dr. Stanton rode along in the ambulance while Phil and his mother followed a few minutes behind.

Phil looked up at the large clock on the wall which seemed to cry out that the time was 3:30 A.M. It had been six long hours since the Smith family arrived at the hospital. Dr. Stanton approached them in the hallway.

"He's conscious, Ann," said the family doctor as he entered the waiting room. Dr. Stanton looked worn out and dark circles shaded his eyes.

"Sam wants to see you and Phil. You may go in for only a few minutes." Dr. Stanton paused, "He's a very sick man, Ann."

Phil held his mother's arm as they entered his father's room. There, lying so still on the bed, was their loved one. They were surprised to find that he did not require oxygen.

62

"Hello, Ann. Hi, Son." A slight smile showed on his twisted face. Phil could see that his mother was fighting back the tears as she patted her husband on the arm.

"Hello, Sam," she said softly. "How do you feel?"

"I feel much better, Honey," he answered in a quiet voice. "I'm sorry I gave you such a scare."

"Don't even think of that," she said, looking at Phil as though she wanted him to take over the conversation.

"You look great, Dad," spoke Phil through a forced smile.

"I've got something I want to tell you, Son," whispered his father. "I've been praying that the Lord would provide for you to go back to school this fall. I know your heart's set on going to candidate school next summer." Sam stopped, closed his eyes a moment and then continued.

"The Lord will provide for you, Phil. Your Mom and I are so proud of you." Again he stopped, breathed deeply and went on. "It's a joy to our hearts to know that our son has been called by the Lord to take the gospel of our blessed Savior to the people of Haiti."

The door opened and Dr. Stanton walked in. "Sorry, Ann, but Sam must have some rest now. He insisted on talking to you tonight, but he can save the rest for another time."

Ann Smith turned, bent over the bed and kissed her husband's forehead. "Good night, Sam. I love you." She then turned her head to keep him from seeing her tears.

"Good night, Ann."

"Good night, Dad," whispered Phil. "I'm praying for you." He could see his father was tiring quickly.

"Good night, Phil. . . . our missionary." A smile spread across his father's face as he closed his eyes. "All things work together for good for those who love God." Phil could not help but notice the peace and contentment reflected in his father's voice.

Ann Smith thought she was dreaming, but it was not a dream. It was really her phone that was ringing. Half asleep, she reached over and picked up the receiver. She noticed the clock's hands showed the time to be 7:10 A.M.

"Hello," she said with her soft voice. The tears began to roll down her face as she listened. "Thank you." She spoke in a whisper as she put the phone down.

Phil had heard the phone ring and came quickly to his mother's room. Her faint sobs told him the answer before he asked. He entered and found her sitting on the edge of the bed. She looked up as he made his way to her side.

"Phil!, Oh, Phil!" she sobbed hardly above a whisper, "the hospital called. Dad went home to be with the Lord this morning."

Phil knelt beside his mother and put his arm around her. His throat felt as if it were tied in one giant knot. "He's home, Mom" he said, wiping his eyes. "Dad will never suffer again."

The following days were difficult ones for Phil and his mother, but they testified over and over again how God's grace was sufficient for their sorrowing hearts. Two weeks after the funeral, the insurance company's check arrived. Phil sat beside his mother as she opened the envelope. Her tears dropped on it as she held it in her lap.

"Here's God's answer, Phil," she said, holding out the check. "Part of this will pay off your school debt, as well as the rest of your tuition." Her face shone radiantly through the glistening tears. "Your father would have wanted it this way. You're his representative, too, Son."

Phil bowed his head in silence and thought of the night he stood beside his father's hospital bed. He knew he'd never forget those precious last words. "Good night, Phil. . . . our missionary."

11

A HAVEN OF REST

NINA KENDRICK

The lush green jungle, which only yesterday seemed so romantic and beautiful, had taken on a sinister air. Virginia sat tensely behind the wheel of the small Renault. In the seat beside her sat her husband, slouched, moaning softly from time to time. She knew Brent was very ill, seeming now to be barely conscious.

The Bradfords had planned this trip to Africa for three years, carefully putting aside every extra penny for their "Great Adventure" account. What a surprise it had been, the day Virginia had confided her lifelong desire to Brent and discovered that since his boyhood he had had the very same desire.

Three weeks ago the excited young couple had embarked on the journey of their lives. As the huge jet swooped in toward the landing field at the large African coastal city, Virginia was reminded of a relief map the children had made in geography class when she was in the sixth grade. The tiny grass-roofed huts she now saw seemed identical to the ones they had made of clay and straw and had placed carefully on the flour, salt and water terrain. She recalled with delight the tiny palm trees they had fashioned and which she now saw duplicated below her. She was so engrossed in the panorama that the bump indicating they had touched down startled her.

Brent was more interested in watching her reactions than in

seeing the scenery himself. Squeezing her hand, the happy young man began to gather their belongings.

For three years every available article and book about the dark continent had been devoured by the two Bradfords. They were unprepared, however, for the noises and smells that now assaulted their senses. Brent with his, "Will you listen to that!" made Virginia turn her head. She silently shook with laughter as two black men in fancy garb passed close by, talking loudly in their local tongue. Everything was so new and exciting that they wished they could see in every direction at once.

Brent and Virginia lost no time in securing a sturdy little car for their trip. Knowing that stores would be few and far between, they carefully bought canned food, bottled water and biscuits in tins. A one-burner camp stove, a couple of pans, two plates, cups, cutlery and a can opener completed their purchases. Within four days, in spite of the language barrier, they were ready to leave the coast for inland Africa.

Two weeks passed as a colorful tapestry of new sights, sounds and tastes met their senses. Never would Virginia forget her first view of the graceful, gangly giraffe. Delicious citrus fruits, pineapple, mangoes and papayas were taste thrills not soon to be forgotten. Dance drums lulled them to sleep at night.

Virginia first noticed that Brent had lost some of his good spirits at the beginning of the third week. One morning he awakened with a severe headache and flushed face, indicating a high fever.

"It's nothing," he insisted. "Probably just the change of water." As the week wore on, Virginia noted nervously that he didn't seem to be improving.

Several days passed in this manner until today when she had to help Brent into the car. And now he sat beside her, unresponsive, with head rolling back and forth on the seat back. Fear gripped her. If only I knew where there was a doctor. I have never felt so alone in all my life. What if he should die?

The miles stretched endlessly before her. The road was rough and full of potholes. She had no way of knowing where she could find help. Brent, in his limited French, had been able to ask directions and take care of purchases. She had no knowledge of French, so was helpless. Minutes stretched into hours.

It was nearing four o'clock that afternoon when the dusty vehicle came to what appeared to be a small store on the right-hand side of the road. At their left was a long drive bordered on either side by tall grass. In desperation, Virginia turned the car into the lane which took her up a gentle incline to the top of a hill. On the right was a brick dwelling with outbuildings at the side. Beyond that was a long building. And farther on, a path led to a cluster of round, grass-roofed huts. In front of her was a large sprawling house with the drive circling in front of a deep veranda. Coral vines dripping bright pink blossoms climbed the side of the porch. Wide-open double doors of dark wood beckoned invitingly to her.

This looks like a haven of rest, she thought. I wonder who lives here? Glancing quickly at Brent, she sprang from the car and ran up the broad, brick steps. Uncertainly, the young girl stopped at the door. In the shadows a small boy regarded her with wide brown eyes.

She saw first the comfortable living room. Dark wood had been used to make the davenport and armchairs. All were covered with bright, plump cushions. Beyond was the dining room furnished with a long table, several chairs and a sideboard all of the same dark wood. Wide windows with filmy curtains gave a spacious look.

Hearing voices, Virginia knocked timidly. Immediately a slender woman, with eyes matching those of the tiny lad outside, appeared at the archway separating the two rooms.

"Why, hello," she greeted cheerfully in English. "Please come in."

"Thank you," Virginia returned, "but my husband is in the car and oh, he is so sick."

The young woman hurried out to the car. She sized up the situation in a glance, and in a strange language gave orders to a young African standing nearby. Running across the compound, he soon reappeared with an older woman in a white uniform. Before Virginia could get over her surprise at seeing a nurse in this out-of-the-way place, Brent was in a comfortable bed in a cool, darkened room.

"Black water fever," the little nurse diagnosed. "Probably no one told you that you should be taking anti-malarial drugs. You, my dear, must start immediately!" The efficient, white-clad figure bustled about, attempting to make Brent comfortable and administering healing drugs.

Anxiety filled Virginia's heart. Just hearing the diagnosis frightened her. Yet, how grateful she was to have found this peaceful place.

After a delicious dinner, the young wife sat in the dark holding her husband's limp hand. From the living room came soft singing. The voices weren't trained or even especially good, but the melody brought tears to her eyes. She had learned at dinner that these fine people were missionaries. They had invited her to join them at their midweek prayer meeting, but she had declined saying she would rather stay with Brent. Now she strained to hear the words of the sweet song:

"I've anchored my soul in the Haven of Rest,
I'll sail the wide seas no more. . . ."

Haven of Rest! That's just what I thought of this home. I wonder what that song means?

As the days passed she began to realize that these folks— Sam and Janie Williams and even tiny Pete, Nurse Florence Anderson and their fourth co-worker, Mary McVey—possessed something that she didn't have. They were like a family, and all shared a simple, warm faith that Virginia envied.

Day by day, under the watchful care of Florence, Brent improved. Life on the mission station flowed around them. Virginia noticed that their days centered around the Word of God. She had never given the Bible much attention, but now she wondered if she had been missing something.

One evening when Brent was able to be up, they sat on the veranda breathing deeply of the air perfumed by huge, white, trumpetlike moonflowers growing on a vine alongside the house.

"Brent, have you noticed how different these folks are?" Virginia asked tentatively.

"Honey, I have. And I think it is a difference we could afford to have," answered the young man. "Let's find out what it is that makes them that way."

Later that same night, Brent and Virginia sat in the living room with Sam and Janie. Peter had long since been in bed.

"How can we ever thank you enough for your good care of us these many days, but especially for what you have given us tonight? We thank you for showing us the way to Jesus. I came here with black water fever, but we both leave with faith in Christ."

Virginia squeezed her husband's hand and said softly, "At last I know what the 'Haven of Rest' really means!"

12

THE FLOUR THIEF

V. BEN KENDRICK

"I don't understand it, Bob. It's impossible for me to use that much flour in a week's time."

Cathy Andrews stood in the doorway of her little red brick house. She had just returned home from her teen-age girls class to find her supply of flour nearly gone. The last time she baked, there was at least ten or more pounds left in the tin.

"I don't know what to make of it, Cathy," said Bob Drake, the mission station superintendent, as he studied her frustrated look. "I'm sure it is one of your house boys."

"You may be right, Bob, but I don't even want to think of that. Mark and Steven have worked for me for fifteen years and I've never missed one thing in all that time." Cathy wiped a tear from her eye. "Why should I suspect either of them now?"

That evening as Bob and Jean sat at the dinner table, the subject of the missing flour was the main conversation.

"And to think," said Bob as he sipped at his coffee, "that such a thing should come up just when we are in the midst of our Annual Bible Conference. It sure could develop into a bad situation if either Mark or Steven are involved in the theft of Cathy's flour."

"What you you mean, Bob?" questioned Jean.

"Well, the spirit of the conference has been great. Every day thus far, we have heard tremendous testimonies of the Lord's blessings in the work. Now, if all of a sudden it is found out that either Mark or Steven is stealing, it would cause a lot of grief and heartache among the believers. Both of those men are loved and respected in this entire area."

"I really don't think Mark or Steven would steal the flour," said Jean as she poured Bob another cup of coffee. "I think it is someone who is nearby and who knows when Cathy leaves for class."

"But the two house boys are there nearly all the time," interjected Bob.

"Well, not all the time," answered his young wife. "There are times when Mark goes to the market and Steven is outside hanging up the wash."

"I hope you're right, Jean, but right now we must assume that it is either Mark or Steven since they have access to the flour all day long."

The next afternoon, Bob and Jean went into town to do some shopping for the conference. They drove slowly by the marketplace looking for a place to park. Suddenly Bob stopped the pickup and pointed to the bread section.

"Jean! Do you see what I see? Isn't that Esther, Mark's daughter, selling bread?"

"Oh, Bob," gasped Jean, "it is Esther and she has a good supply of bread, too."

The trip back to the mission station was unusually quiet as the thought of what they had seen lay heavily upon the young couple's hearts. As Bob turned into the station's driveway, he spotted Cathy returning home from her afternoon class.

"Are you sure it was Esther and not some other girl, Bob?" Cathy's face showed unbelief written all over it.

"I'm positive, Cathy. Jean saw her too. We know it was Esther."

"Let's not do anything about it now, Bob. I think we should wait a few days. I will keep my eyes open for anything that looks suspicious."

Later that afternoon at church, Mark stood and told how the Lord had blessed his family. He thanked the Lord for finances which he had received in recent days and which made it possible for him to buy a new bicycle. As he spoke, Bob and Jean glanced over at Cathy. Her face reflected the hurt that was deep inside her.

On their way home after the service, Jean turned and looked at Bob. "Honey, what has happened to Mark? He acts as though nothing is wrong."

"Beats me, Jean. How can a guy, who has walked with the Lord for so many years, just simply turn his back upon Him like that? And to think that he even gives the Lord the credit for helping him get that kind of money."

After dinner, the missionaries returned to the church for the evening meeting. It was difficult for Jean to even concentrate on the message as she thought of seeing Esther that afternoon and later, hearing Mark thank the Lord for the funds he recently received. That night as Bob and Jean prayed together, Jean could not hold back the tears.

"How could Mark do such a thing?" she thought to herself. Sleep came late for the young missionaries as they talked about their disappointment in Mark.

The early African sun peeped over the distant hill, sending its bright beams across the little mission station. Bob, who always arose early, heard a noise behind him on the path. "Good morning, Mr. Drake," came a familiar voice. Bob turned to see Mark hurrying towards him holding something in his hand. "Mr. Drake, I have some money here that I would like for you to give to someone for me."

Bob's knees felt weak. Should I say something to Mark? he thought. Would it be right for me to ask him where he got the money? What about the stolen flour?

Mark waited for Bob's answer.

The young missionary then looked at Mark. "Why do you want me to give the money to someone, Mark? Why don't you do it yourself?"

Mark's dark brown eyes met those of Bob. "Well, it's like

this, Mr. Drake. I have had this money for two weeks now and was going to buy a pair of pants and a shirt. Yesterday after the afternoon service, I overheard Pastor Paul tell his wife that he needed shoes. The Lord spoke to my heart as I left the church and He told me to give this money to the pastor to buy shoes. I figured you were the best one to give it to him. That is one of the reasons I met you here on the path this morning."

Mark placed the money in Bob's hand.

"Mark!" said Bob, surprised to hear his own voice, "I have something to ask you. I hope you won't think I'm prying into your business, Mark, but I heard your testimony in the service yesterday about having these funds. I understand, too, that you recently bought a new bicycle."

A serious look spread over Mark's face as he listened to his friend.

Bob hesitated and then spoke again. "Mark, please forgive me for asking you this very personal question, but where did you get all this money?"

The surprised African didn't know that Bob was thinking about the stolen flour. He did, however, sense that his beloved missionary was suspicious of something.

"Mr. Drake," said Mark as he stepped toward Bob, "being as poor as we are, you have every reason to ask such a question. Please don't feel bad about it."

The smile on Mark's face reassured Bob who was beginning to feel better even though he had not yet heard what Mark had to say.

"It's a long story, but I will try to tell it to you quickly. My Uncle Bada, who lived in the village of Donga, died about a month ago. Several years ago, he borrowed some money from my father and just before my father died, he told my uncle to pay the loan to me. For some reason, Uncle Bada did not pay me that money right away. When Uncle knew that he was going to die, he told my aunt that he wanted her to sell his gun and shells as well as his motorbike, and give the funds to me. Well, they sold for a very good price and I received the money from my aunt two weeks ago. Mr. Drake, I've never had so much money at one time. I even want to help the church in its new roof project."

"Thank you, Mark, for telling me this. I must confess that I was afraid that Satan had tempted you to steal Miss Cathy's flour. When I saw Esther selling bread in the market place, I was sure that it was made from the stolen flour."

Mark broke out into a big smile and grabbed Bob's hand. "Well, Mr. Drake, you sure had a good case, and I can see why you believed what you did. By the way, Esther was helping her cousin. My brother-in-law is now baking bread for a living."

Bob's face became serious again. "Mark, who could the flour thief be?"

"Well, that's the other reason I wanted to see you the first thing this morning. Miss Cathy hired a new gardener several weeks ago."

"Do you mean John?" interrupted Bob.

"Yes, I mean John," answered Mark nodding his head. "This past week, Steven and I have suspected John of stealing the flour but could not catch him in the act."

"Is he a Christian, Mark?"

"When he came for a job, he told Miss Cathy that he was a believer. In fact, he even quoted her some Scripture verses. Well, last night, I found him standing outside the church listening to the message. I asked him to go in but he said he had to leave early and didn't want to disturb the service. He stayed through the entire message and when the invitation was given, I saw him bow his head and start for the village. I followed him and caught up with him about halfway home. In talking to him, Mr. Drake, I sensed that he was very much afraid."

"Afraid of what?" asked Bob.

"Afraid to die and meet God. He told me that he was not a Christian and that he lied to get the job as gardener. He also said that he had been entering Miss Cathy's house and stealing her flour. To make a long story short, John accepted the Lord and is coming this morning to confess what he has done to Miss Cathy. He plans to pay her back for all the flour he stole from her. He's a changed boy, Mr. Drake."

"Praise the Lord, Mark," said Bob as he reached out to shake his African brother's hand.

"Yes, praise the Lord," responded Mark. "Once again, we have seen the miraculous power of God manifest through the preaching of His Word."

The two friends shook hands again and parted. As Bob headed home, he knew that his breakfast would taste especially good to him after his conversation with Mark.

13

PRODIGAL TWINS

V. BEN KENDRICK

Ann glanced at the Sunday school paper she had received in church. A tiny chill rippled through her. "If I didn't know better," she said, "I would think the author was writing about me."

It had been three weeks since Ann had returned home after being away for nearly two months. She found it difficult to think of all she had gone through during the past twelve weeks. Ann knew it took a miracle for the Lord to redirect her steps and bring her back to her family.

As she looked at the illustration on the Sunday school paper, she saw herself as the girl in the story. The drawing blurred as tears filled her eyes.

"Father," she prayed, "thank You for Your faithfulness. Thank You for bringing me back home."

"It's time to eat, Ann," called her mother, standing at the foot of the stairs. "The food is on the table, Honey."

"I'll be right down, Mom" answered Ann. She glanced at herself in the mirror. How happy she was to be back home with her parents. Even more important, that she was back in fellowship with her Lord.

"Thank you, Lord," she whispered, starting down the

stairs. That afternoon, after the dishes were put away, Ann sat in the front room reading when the telephone rang.

"I'll get it, Mom," she called, hurrying across the room. "It's Mrs. Birch. She wants me to come over this afternoon for a little while. She says Cynthia is home from college for the day and would like to talk with me."

Martha Herrman smiled, indicating her joy in the invitation.

"I'll be right over, Mrs. Birch," responded Ann, putting the receiver down.

"Honey," said her mother, "Cynthia is out of fellowship with the Lord." Ann noted a strain of grief in her mother's voice. "You'll find she's not the same girl who went forward in church last year when she dedicated her life to the Lord for missions."

"Oh, Mom," said Ann, the tears welling up, "I know so well what she is going through. Who would have thought three weeks ago that Ann Herrman would be in any condition to help anyone?"

Martha Herrman put her arms around her daughter. "We just kept trusting the Lord, Honey. His promises are as strong as His very existence. We're so thankful He brought you back to Himself."

"I'll be back in time for church, Mom," called Ann as she went out the door. The Sunday school paper was still clutched in her hand.

Ann felt scared as she rang the doorbell of the Birch home. It seemed only seconds until the door opened. There before her stood Cynthia, her friend since childhood days. They greeted each other with a hug, and Ann stepped inside. She had not seen Cynthia since she went away to school. Mrs. Birch greeted Ann warmly and quietly left the room.

"I'm so glad you could come over, Ann. I wanted to share with you some of the neat things going on at college. Mom's gone upstairs so we have privacy to talk."

Ann sat patiently listening to Cynthia as she related one story after another . . . the main theme being boys and parties.

"Hey, wait a minute!" said Cynthia after a solid half hour of chatter. "I've been doing all the talking. Now it's your turn, Ann.

How about telling me about yourself? One of the kids told me you split a couple of months ago, but came home for some reason. Where did you go? Tell me about all those guys you met."

Ann felt the opportunity had come for her to tell Cynthia of the change that had taken place in her life. She silently asked the Lord to give her just the right words to say.

"Yes, I did leave home for about two months," began Ann. "I wanted freedom. I didn't want to be put into anyone's mold, especially the religious mold of my parents. I figured I was a person, too, and wanted to live my own life . . . away from them."

A knowing smile appeared on Cynthia's face.

"At first I even seemed to enjoy the independence of being alone. I got a job in a restaurant in St. Louis and was sure I had found what I was looking for. No more church and no more parents around to hassle me. I don't want to go into detail, Cynthia, but I was out to have a good time, and to get it any way I could. Drinking, wild parties and even drugs became a daily thing for me."

Cynthia sat quietly listening to Ann as she unfolded her story.

"I called my parents only one time to tell them that I was all right, but other than that, there was no communication between us. It was impossible for them to write or even call me. I refused to tell them where I was. Since I've been home I have realized what terrible agony I've caused my parents." Ann paused as her voice broke. "I'm sure of one thing, Cynthia, it is easier for us to go our own ways and forget our parents than it is for them to forget us, their children. I find this true of our relationship with the Lord, too."

Cynthia opened her mouth to say something, but remained silent.

"It was during my last week away from home when the accident happened. I was out with Bob, a married man who had two children. He told his wife he was going bowling with some of the men at the office, but instead went out with me."

Ann paused and looked at the floor. "You know, Cynthia, I have found that it is so easy to rationalize anything we want to do, whether it is right or wrong. Bob told me he had an argument with his wife that day. I figured he was a nice guy and needed cheering up. We were driving along a country road that afternoon. All of a sudden a little boy ran out of the bushes onto the road. Bob slammed on the brakes, but it was too late. The car left the road and hit a tree. The door on my side opened and I was thrown out onto the grass. The car then rolled down the embankment. It finally stopped, resting on its top about forty feet below. Bob crawled out unhurt." Ann buried her face in her hands. "Cynthia," she cried, "I'll never forget seeing that little boy lying lifeless alongside the road. The police cleared Bob of any charges."

Ann put her hand on Cynthia's arm. "God really spoke to my heart right there. I cried to Him for forgiveness. I promised I would live the rest of my life for Him."

"Look," said Cynthia, "it wasn't your fault. Why punish yourself?"

"I'm not punishing myself," responded Ann. "I simply realized there is more to life than what I was doing. When Jesus died, He died not only to give us everlasting life, but also to purchase these bodies of ours that we may be of service to Him. I'm ashamed of what I've done, Cynthia. Life is too precious to use it for things which really don't count for Christ."

"I haven't thought too much about those things," said Cynthia. "I know that Christ is the One Who really counts." She slowly dropped her head into her hands. "What's happened to me, Ann? The more you talked to me today, the more I realized that something's wrong. Do you remember that night, Ann, when we went forward and gave our lives to the Lord?"

"I remember, Cynthia," responded Ann, as she wiped away a tear. "I often think of the little plaque Mom has on the wall in the living room. 'Only one life 'twill soon be passed. Only what's done for Christ will last.' "

Within minutes the two girls knelt beside each other. "Dear Father," prayed Cynthia, "I've sinned against You. Please forgive me, Lord. Help me to live the rest of my life for You."

After the girl finished praying, Cynthia's eyes sparkled with tears. "I feel like the Prodigal who returned."

"We both are returned prodigals," answered Ann. "I guess we could call ourselves the Prodigal Twins."

Cynthia put her arm around her friend. "Thank the Lord for His love and patience, and for the love of our parents, too," said Ann. "It's been a wonderful afternoon!

"I'd better be going, Cynthia," she added. "I told Mom I would be home in time to go to church with her and Dad."

Cynthia walked over to the stairway. Unknown to her, her mother had spent the afternoon on her knees praying for her daughter.

"Mom!" she called, "We're going to be late for church if you don't hurry."

Jane Birch arose from the side of her bed. Cynthia's voice sounded different. She knew God had answered her prayers.

"Thank You, Lord," whispered Ann as she left the Birch home. On the way out, she dropped her Sunday school paper on the dining room table. Cynthia, too, would identify with the girl in the story.

14

LEPROSY AND GOD'S WILL

V. BEN KENDRICK

"The leprosy colony! Why, we can't go there to work. One of us might get that terrible disease."

The words of the recent Bible school graduate left Sam speechless. "But . . . but . . . those people are lost, too, Banga. They need to hear the gospel and besides, there are already believers there."

As he spoke, the veteran missionary noticed the troubled look in the African's eyes. He sensed that Banga was upset from the way he had spoken.

Sam continued. "Why just this week we received another letter from the colony asking for someone to come and teach them God's Word."

Banga stood up. "I agree, Mr. Mack, that someone should go out to the colony but that someone is not me. I know what that disease can do to a person's body. I'm not going to get near that place."

Sam Mack watched until Banga had disappeared around the hedge at the end of the driveway. The missionary then bowed his head. "Father, speak to Banga concerning the need at the colony. Help him, Lord, to give You the proper place in his life."

Upon entering the house, Sam shared with Barbara his conversation with Banga. "I just couldn't believe his attitude, Honey. Why, all of us are exposed to leprosy every day here at the mission station. Dorothy has at least fifty leprosy patients who come to the dispensary regularly for medicine."

"You're right, Sam," responded Barbara. "Dorothy has been exposed to it for years and she hasn't caught it yet."

That night Sam and Barbara invited the station nurse, Dorothy Mason, over for the evening meal. Being the only single lady on the station, Dorothy spent a good deal of her spare time with the Macks. They often had meals together.

The missionary nurse was surprised as well to hear what Banga had said to Sam. "Has he indicated to you where he would like to work?" asked Dorothy.

"That's the thing," answered Sam. "It's been a month since graduation and Banga and Kunda haven't shown any effort to find a place to work. It's not that there aren't any places to go. Why, the requests for a worker keep coming weekly from the believers at the leprosy colony. The last time I was there I told them that we would pray with them that God would provide a worker."

"Well, there's a couple here," added Barbara.

"That's right," said Sam, "but with no desire to go there. And besides, he's afraid to go to the colony for fear he'll get leprosy."

Before Dorothy returned to her house, the three missionaries took time to pray for Banga and Kunda as well as the need at the leprosy colony.

A week later it was time for Sam to make his monthly trip to the colony. He walked over to the nearby village to see if Banga would like to make the one day visit with him. Sam found him in front of his hut with Kunda. The couple stood to greet the missionary and shook his hand.

"Hello, Friends. I've come to ask you something."

"Thank you, Mr. Mack," said Banga, placing a small wooden stool on the ground in front of the missionary. "What do you have upon your heart?"

82

"I'm going to the colony tomorrow for the day, and I was wondering if you would like to go with me. We will be back home by evening."

The African was silent for a moment and then spoke slowly. "Thank you, Mr. Mack, but I was planning to work in my garden tomorrow. I've just planted a large piece of ground. Maybe some other time."

Sam looked at Banga as he spoke. "I thought that if you saw the need at the colony, it would give you and Kunda something to pray about. I know you are asking the Lord to show you where to go to work for Him."

"Well, thank you, Mr. Mack," repeated the African, "but like I said, maybe I'll be able to go the next time."

Sam's trip to the colony was the usual blessed experience for him. He spoke twice during the day and before leaving prayed with the believers that God would send someone to teach them His Word.

The weeks passed into months but still Banga and Kunda waited for direction from the Lord. Many more letters arrived from the colony reminding the missionaries of the great need and asking them to continue to pray that someone would come.

By this time, Banga had become deeply involved in his gardening. He sold his products in the town market and was beginning to make a good income. The missionaries became increasingly concerned as the African couple drifted farther away from the Lord. Their hearts were heavy to see four years of Bible school training go unused. As they sat on the veranda late one afternoon a government medical truck drove into the mission compound. The three missionaries went out to meet their guests.

"I'm looking for Miss Mason," spoke the man in charge of the medical unit.

Dorothy held out her hand for the usual handshake. "I'm Dorothy Mason. What can I do for you?"

"Miss Mason," continued the African health official, "we want to examine the people of this area for leprosy, and I understand you are very experienced in dealing with that disease. Would you be so kind as to work with us for a couple of days? If you wish, we can set up our equipment right across the road from your dispensary."

"I would be delighted to do what I can. Let me know what you want me to do," answered the nurse.

The official then told the missionaries how the government planned to enlarge the leprosy colony and that all confirmed leprosy patients would be sent to the colony.

"We want to stamp out the disease, and the only way we can do it is to send everyone with it to the colony."

The next day people by the hundreds made their way to the temporary medical camp. Dorothy was given the task of examining the women. One by one they passed by her table. She heard a familiar voice and looked up to see Kunda looking at her.

"Hello, Kunda," said the nurse, smiling. "How are you today?"

"I'm all right, I think," she answered hesitantly.

Dorothy knew that something was troubling the woman. Within minutes she discovered a spot on Kunda's side. The American nurse's experience in treating leprosy made it easy for her to recognize the disease. Dorothy's look confirmed Kunda's fears. She threw her arms around the missionary.

"Oh, Miss Mason," she cried. "I'm going to have to leave my family and go to live in the colony."

Dorothy tried to comfort her friend. "The Lord knows all about you, Kunda. He'll work everything out for you somehow. Trust Him, dear Kunda. Trust Him."

Banga was stunned when his wife told him she had leprosy. Suddenly his garden business seemed worthless and meaningless. He knew that Kunda would be sent to the colony, leaving him and the children behind. Tears came to his eyes and trickled down his face.

"Kunda, my wife, a leper!" cried Banga to himself. Slowly he slipped to his knees. "Dear Father," he prayed, "I've sinned against You. I've closed my ears to Your call. I've gone my own way. Father, please forgive me."

Kunda knelt down beside her husband. The tears coursed

down her face as she prayed. "Dear Lord, thank You for my leprosy. We wouldn't listen to You when you tried to talk to us. We're ready to listen now, Father. Thank You for giving us direction."

Two days later, Banga and Kunda loaded their possessions into a government truck. Sam and Barbara and Dorothy stood talking with Banga and Kunda. The couple were excited over the latest event in their lives.

"I haven't been this happy since Bible school graduation, Mr. Mack." spoke Banga. "I can't wait until we get to the colony and begin our ministry."

Sam prayed for the little family before they boarded the truck. Kunda hugged Barbara and Dorothy. "Good-bye my sisters," she said, looking at them through her tears. "Thank you for your love and prayers."

The missionaries waved until the truck was out of sight. Barbara noticed a tear trickle down Sam's face. His voice showed his emotion as he spoke.

"Thank the Lord for His faithfulness. It took a case of leprosy to move Banga and Kunda to the colony, but they're finally happy and in God's will."

15

"GIVE YE THEM TO EAT"

V. BEN KENDRICK

Laura watched the tiny white-haired woman as she stood motionless on the platform. Her slightly bent, frail body appeared to be frozen in place. Now and then a trace of a smile could be seen on her aged face.

Rev. Toms' deep, clear voice could be easily heard throughout the large auditorium. "Dear friends, we have a special blessing in store for us today. It is our privilege to have one of God's choice servants with us. Miss Mary Stern comes with an outstanding testimony of God's faithfulness."

Laura turned to her friend, Ann Price, sitting beside her. "A privilege?" she whispered in a sarcastic voice. "She looks like someone right out of the Dark Ages."

Ann looked straight ahead. She didn't want to encourage Laura in her sarcasm and thought it best to ignore the remark. She had noticed a change in Laura the past few weeks. It was only that week that Ann found out that her friend had been secretly dating an unsaved boy. She had not said anything to Laura, but was praying for her.

Mary Stern stepped up to the microphone which was attached to the pulpit. Only the top of her shoulders and head were visible. Her thin hands gripped the side of the broad pulpit. She waited a moment and then began to speak.

"I thank God I'm alive today." She stopped to swallow and then continued. "It's a miracle that I am able to be here. You see, dear friends, I was a prisoner for nearly three years in a Japanese prison camp."

The words 'prison camp' caught Laura's attention. She stared ahead at the little old lady, straining to hear every word of the trembling voice.

"Rumors were about that enemy soldiers were nearby, but we didn't know where to hide. It was decided that it would be best to stay in our homes on the mission station. I shall never forget the day they came. It was about four o'clock in the afternoon and I had just come into the house. I heard guns shooting and men shouting. I looked out the window just in time to see the soldiers coming across the front yard. My heart skipped a beat and fear immediately gripped me. My entire body became numb. The Lord immediately gave me the verse in Isaiah 41:10, 'Fear thou not;.for I am with thee: be not dismayed; for I am thy God: I will strengthen thee; yea, I will help thee; yea, I will uphold thee with the right hand of my righteousness.'

"The door burst open and a number of soldiers rushed into the room with their guns lifted ready to shoot. The looks on their faces were indescribable when they saw a little old lady facing them. One of them spoke to me but I didn't understand a word of what he was saying. I pointed to myself and lifted one finger to show that I was the only one in the house. I guess they either didn't believe me or didn't understand because while two of them held their guns on me the others searched the house.

"A few minutes later, I was pushed out the door where I saw my four co-workers standing in the middle of the mission compound. One of the men had a gash on the side of his face—the result of a blow by one of the soldiers with the butt of a rifle. We were lined up in a single file and told to start walking toward a small path which led into the jungle.

" 'They're going to kill us,' I heard one of the missionaries say in a whisper. In spite of the horrible thought of being shot, God flooded my heart with His perfect peace. I felt like singing praises to the Lord."

Laura leaned over and spoke softly to Ann. "She is really something. I couldn't be that brave."

Ann smiled at her friend's remark. She prayed in her heart that God would use the veteran missionary's testimony to speak to Laura.

As Mary Stern continued, the entire congregation sat spellbound and listened to every word.

"We walked for two days with very little food or water. Every now and then the soldiers would push us into the underbrush fearing we would be spotted by low flying planes. Huge blisters appeared on my feet. When the blisters broke, they caused my feet to become very sore. After much walking and suffering, we finally reached an area enclosed by barbed wire. Armed guards seemed to be everywhere. A crude gate was pulled open, and we were pushed into the mass of half-starved, sick people. The stench was unbearable. Privacy was unheard of, and for the first time in my life, I felt like I wanted to die."

Ann noticed Laura wiping a tear from her eye.

The veteran missionary took a sip of water from the glass on the pulpit. "I could feel myself growing weaker with each new day. I lost all trace of time. Several of the prisoners scratched out calendars on the ground which they carefully guarded. It was one way for them to pass the time and concentrate on something other than their helpless condition.

"It was a daily event for the guards to stand near the fence with large pans of food. They would gorge themselves with all kinds of delicious-looking foods while we were starving. When they were full they would hold the food just out of reach of our bony, outstretched arms. I can still hear the sobbing and pleading of those half-crazed prisoners, begging for a bit of food. After the soldiers had finished eating, they would dump the rest of the food on the ground and crush it into the dirt with their boots."

Mary stopped to get control of her trembling voice. "Each time we heard a truck, we knew that more of our group would be taken, never to be seen again. It was only the Word of God hidden away in my heart that kept me from going out of my mind. I would start with the Book of Genesis and quote as many verses as I could, working my way through the Bible. Since we weren't allowed to sing, I would softly whisper hymn after hymn. God's Word became very precious to me.

"I was sitting on the ground in the corner of the prison yard one day when I heard voices speaking in English. At first I thought I was dreaming, and then I saw a soldier appear out of the nearby bush. I hadn't noticed that our guards had quickly disappeared, leaving the prison camp unattended.

" 'It's all over! someone shouted from outside the prison. 'We've come to set you free!'

"I struggled to my feet; my legs were shaking with weakness. I turned to walk toward the gate which had swung open. I wanted to cry out with joy, but there was no sound. Before I realized what was happening, I was swept off my feet and lifted into the arms of a young American soldier.

" 'Mom, it's all over! You're free. The war is over. We've won the victory!'

"I can't begin to tell you of the joy that swept over that prison camp that day. The sight of our American soldiers was beyond description. The young soldier carried me out of the camp where medical personnel had already begun to examine the prisoners. Even though I was suffering badly from starvation, the sight of the soldiers and the thought of being free gave me new strength. After a few weeks of hospital care, I returned to the United States to continue my recuperation."

The elderly missionary stopped and stared out over the congregation. Tears began to trickle down her wrinkled face.

"Friends, the story which I have just related is a picture of the church today. We are guilty of gorging ourselves with God's Word while others are spiritually starving to death. God says in His Word, 'Give ye them to eat.' "

The people sat with their eyes fixed on the tiny woman.

"The world is filled with those bound in Satan's prison camp. There are millions who have not yet heard the good news that Christ died to set them free . . . that the victory has been won."

Her thin arm stretched out toward the congregation. "Perhaps there is someone here today whom God wants to carry the good news of the cross to those prisoners of sin. My friend, would you be that messenger of life?"

Laura's heart ached within her. She knew she was not living for the Lord. She dabbed at her eyes, finding it impossible to stop the flow of tears. As the invitation hymn was sung, Pastor Toms stood at the front of the auditorium. Laura slipped out of her seat and walked quickly down the aisle where she was met by the minister.

"Pastor," she sobbed softly, "God has spoken to my heart today. My life belongs to the Lord. I'm giving it to Him now for missionary service."

The pastor spoke with Laura for a few moments and then motioned for Mary to go with her to one of the side rooms. Once inside, Laura shared her decision with the older missionary.

"When you were introduced, I told my girlfriend that you belonged in the Dark Ages," she said, half crying and half laughing. "You said just what I needed to hear today. I'm so glad you came. Thank you."

Mary Stern reached over and took Laura's hand. "Always remember God's command, Laura. 'Give ye them to eat.' "

As the two women prayed, Ann sat waiting in the back of the auditorium for her friend . . . praising the Lord for what He had done that morning in Laura's heart.

16

THAT CANTANKEROUS OLD MACHINE!

NINA KENDRICK

"This old washer!" Nan impatiently kicked at the motor which, much to her surprise, roared into activity. "Humph, I should have kicked you sooner!"

Wash day! How she hated it. She never knew if the gasoline motor would start or not. The rickety old washer was temperamental and often sputtered and coughed its way into doubtful service. The old washer, bought from some retiring missionaries, was set on a cement slab under a sprawling mango tree. When not in use, it was covered with an old plastic sheet secured with stones.

As if by magic, the roar produced a ring of shiny black faces, each with a pair of huge black eyes. Today she saw a new face.

"Hello there," she said. "What is your name?"

Nan bent closer to hear the quiet voice in the din of the machine. "My name is Samuel. I have come to see the big animal that roars. My friends say it washes the white man's clothes!"

"Right," smiled Nan. "Watch now while this animal takes the water out of the clothes."

With that, she started shoving towels through the wringer into the rinse water. Samuel, a boy of about sixteen, clapped his hands. And with a typical, "Eh, eh, eh," he danced up and down.

No doubt, she thought, he is remembering how his mother beats the clothes on a rock to get them clean and with strong hands wrings the water from them. Samuel watched in wonder as Alphonse, her houseboy, took the basket of clothes and hung them on the line. Nan knew that Samuel's mother would have hung them on a bush to dry.

"Samuel," the missionary's soft voice brought the young fellow back from his reverie. "This machine is washing our clothes nice and clean. Did you know that God sent His Son to wash our hearts clean in His blood?"

Immediately the light went out of Samuel's face, and his eyes became wary. The change was so sudden that Nan was taken off guard. She was totally unprepared for the hostility that suddenly erupted from this quiet, polite boy.

"I didn't come here to hear about the white man's God." He spat the words out. Then turning, he stalked abruptly away.

The others watched silently as the tall youth strode along the path to the village. No one spoke for several minutes.

Finally, Nan broke the silence. "What did I say that made him so angry?"

Boutangara, the self-appointed spokesman for the group, began, "Don't feel badly, Mama. A few weeks ago Samuel's mother became very sick. The people in her village finally went to get the nurse from the mission station north of us. Miss Barlow did all she could, and all the Christians prayed, but Samuel's mother died. It wasn't the nurse's fault. They just waited too long before going for her. Samuel thinks our God can't hear. He thinks God doesn't care about him. He even wonders if there is a God. After his mother died, he came to our village to live with his brother. Today he came here because he heard the roar of the big animal." Suddenly embarassed by this long speech, Boutangara slid to the back of the little group.

Nan finished the wash mechanically, then walked across the open space to the back door of her little home. Without turning, but knowing full well that the little group had silently followed her, she said quietly, "We'll pray for Samuel. With

92

God's help we'll make him see that the Lord does care about him." Opening the door, she slipped inside the house.

During the intervening weeks Samuel was never far from Nan's thoughts. The bitterness of one so young had affected her deeply. Together with her husband Peter and five-year-old Judy, she prayed daily for Samuel.

Each wash day Nan looked around the circle of faces hoping to see Samuel's face. Three weeks passed.

On the fourth Monday, pouring rain prevented the usual weekly wash. But when Nan awoke on Tuesday bright sunlight filtered through the open window, and she could smell wood smoke. Knowing that Alphonse had already started to heat the wash water, she began mentally to fight the battle of the gasoline motor.

As usual, there was not a person to be seen as she and Judy went outside. She groaned as she saw the large pile of clothes. Even one extra day added much to the laundry when one lived in the tropics. Within the inner parts of its greasy mechanical brain, the motor decided to cooperate. It clamored deafeningly into instant usefulness.

With the noise, the inevitable circle of awed faces appeared. A familiar figure stood off to the side. Nan went about her work, appearing not to see Samuel as he inched closer and closer. She felt as though she should hold her breath lest the fragile hold be broken. Nevertheless, she chatted as usual with the little group.

When the last pair of socks was put through the wringer, Nan called for Judy who was playing nearby, and they headed for the back door.

She had gone only a few steps when a voice called, "Please, Mama, may I talk to you?"

She turned to face Samuel and realized he was different from the last time she had seen him. Instead of bitterness in his face, she now saw longing.

"Of course, Samuel. Come over to the house, and we can talk where it is quiet." Breathing a prayer for guidance, Nan invited the now trembling boy into the cool living room. "What did you want to talk to me about, Son?" she asked gently.

Then almost incoherent words tumbled out. After a struggle to regain his composure, he was able to tell her his story. Much of it she had already learned from the other young people but none of them knew the torment he had gone through since they had last been together.

After he left that day, Samuel had wandered aimlessly for several hours, wondering why he had talked to the missionary lady that way. His mother had loved the God that she did. His heart hurt him when he remembered how his mother had wanted him to believe too. He had only laughed, telling her that it was all right for old people to believe like that, but strong young men like himself had no need for such beliefs. He could still see the pain in her kind face. Each time he had come near to seeking help during those weeks, Satan would set up another barrier. Each Monday morning when he heard the washing machine motor start, he was reminded that the help he needed could be found there at the mission station. He longed for relief but feared being called a weakling.

The previous Saturday he had decided to visit friends in a village about an hour's walk away. All weekend he sought to forget his troublesome thoughts. He decided to stay until Tuesday morning because a friend offered him a ride back in an old pickup. His friend had deposited him directly in front of the gate leading to the mission compound just as the noisy motor started. It was Tuesday but he hadn't escaped after all! Like a magnet, the drone of the motor led him into the yard of the missionary.

Peter had slipped into the room during the recital. He and Nan were now smiling in wonder at God's unerring timing. Step by step Samuel was shown the plan of salvation. And before they had even finished, he interrupted with the announcement, "I want my heart washed clean in the blood of Jesus, just as the animal washes Mama's clothes clean every week."

They all bowed their heads while Samuel asked the Lord to wash away his sins in Jesus' blood and to become his Savior.

Three happy people agreed when Nan exclaimed, "Just think of that! God can even use a cantankerous old washing machine to bring people to Himself!"

94

17

THE COLLISION

V. BEN KENDRICK

Randy glanced over his shoulder as he rounded second base. He could see the center fielder converging on the ball that stopped rolling at the bottom of the fence. His left foot hit the inside corner of the third base bag as he continued to circle the bases.

"Slide, Randy!" yelled the next batter, stretching out his hands with the palms down. "Hit the dirt!"

The high school senior slid low and hard. He felt the catcher's shin guard strike against the side of his face. For a moment, everything went black. Then he heard the umpire's voice.

"You're out!" shouted the man in the blue uniform, bending over the base runner.

Randy reached up to feel his numbed face. When he took his hand away, it was covered with blood. The collision with the shin guard had left a deep gash under his right eye. Several teammates rushed to help him.

"Easy, Preacher," said one of the players as he helped Randy to his feet. "That was a bad collision you had."

Coach Bender met his star player halfway to the dugout. "That's a bad cut you have there, Randy. I'll have Dr. Edwards take you right over to the hospital for X rays."

"But, Coach," said Randy, "this is our last game. I've been

looking forward to playing Butler ever since they beat us in the opening game."

A smile appeared on Randy's swollen, bloody face. "Maybe we can tape it shut. I sure don't want to leave the game now."

"You drove in the tie breaking run, Randy. If Jim's fast ball is working for him, I think we can hold those Bull Dogs for the rest of the game."

The high school senior sat in silence as the team's doctor drove him to the hospital. The middle-aged physician had seen many athletes come and go during his twenty-two years at Pompton High, but he had never seen anyone with the talent and determination of Randy Wood. He sensed the player's disappointment and didn't want to force a conversation with him. Finally, Randy broke the silence.

"I appreciate you taking me to the hospital, Dr. Edwards. I know it's the only thing to do, but I really wanted to stay in that game."

"I know that, Randy," responded the doctor, "but the sooner we get that cut taken care of, the better. Besides, you did drive in the lead run. That should be enough insurance for Jim Green.

"But . . . but, that's the problem, Dr. Edwards." Randy found it difficult to say what was bothering him.

"What do you mean, Randy?" asked the team doctor. "What problem are you talking about? Is there something wrong with Jim?" Dr. Edwards looked puzzled as he glanced across the seat at his patient.

"I know this will sound way out, Dr. Edwards, but Jim says that he's an atheist." Randy's face winced with pain as he spoke. "Jim is angry with me. He told me that I had no right to share my faith in Christ with others. He said that I was forcing my belief on people by witnessing to them."

"But we all have the right to share with others what we think is good," said the doctor. "I know you better than that, Randy. You aren't the kind to force your religion on anyone."

Randy was glad to hear Dr. Edwards' encouraging words.

He was sure the doctor wasn't a Christian and he felt convicted that he had not witnessed to him before.

"This week," continued Randy, "Jim came to me and told me that I should not witness to any more of the students. He said his girlfriend had attended one of our student fellowships and got the weird idea that the Bible is God's Word. She also told Jim that Jesus, God's Son, died on the cross for her sins."

Dr. Edwards turned the car into the hospital driveway. "Well, here we are, Randy. Maybe we can continue this conversation after we take care of that cut."

"We can't wait, Dr. Edwards," said Randy, excitedly. "Jim has threatened to throw the game to Butler to keep us from winning the league championship."

"He what?" questioned the doctor.

"He said that he would throw the game today."

"But why would he do that?" asked Dr. Edwards.

"To keep the team from winning the championship. You see, Dr. Edwards, I'm the team captain. He feels that this is the best way to get back at me for my Christian testimony."

"Why didn't you tell this to Coach Bender?"

Randy lifted his hand to the ice pack. "Because I wanted to wait and see if Jim would really try to throw the game. If I saw anything suspicious, I then planned to tell the coach."

"Now I see why you didn't want to leave," said the doctor. "I'll call the field and see how the game is coming."

When Dr. Edwards stepped from the phone booth, Randy knew something was wrong.

"I'm afraid you are right, Randy. Jim Green walked three in a row and wild pitched the tying run home. Coach Bender is on the mound with him now."

"Call the field again, Dr. Edwards," said Randy, almost pleading. "There's a temporary phone in the dugout. I must speak with Coach Bender."

Within minutes Randy heard his coach's voice. "Hello."

"Coach, this is Randy. Can you call time again? Send someone out to the mound to talk with Jim. Stall somehow. I need to tell you something.

The high school coach had great confidence in the team's captain and without hesitating, called for time. He motioned to one of the substitute players on the bench.

"Pete, go out there and talk with him. Ask him if he's tired. Stay out there as long as possible."

Coach Bender turned to the phone. "Go ahead, Randy, but make it fast. The umpires won't wait very long."

Randy explained quickly to his coach why Jim was pitching so badly.

"But who can we put in there to pitch?" asked the coach. "Sam is home sick with the flu and Tom has a sore arm."

"Bring in Brent Walker from centerfield. He can't throw breaking balls but he does have a good fast ball and he's very accurate."

"Good suggestion, Randy, I'll put Pete in centerfield."

Jim Green was surprised when he was taken from the game. He knew he was the only available pitcher, and it was a real put-down for him to see Brent Walker take over on the mound.

"He's no pitcher, Coach. They'll hit him all over the place," said the angry ball player.

"Brent will do all right, Jim. I'm not worried about him. At least he'll be honest in playing the game."

The ousted pitcher cast a sheepish look toward his coach.

Bud Angle, the catcher, chatted with the new pitcher on the mound. "Don't be nervous, Brent. You can throw just as hard, if not harder, than Jim. Remember one thing—aim for my glove and throw as hard as you can."

The opposing batters swung wildly at the zooming fast balls. Now and then one would manage to get a piece of the ball and foul it off. Brent retired the first three batters he faced. His heart beat wildly with excitement as he returned to the bench.

In the bottom of the eighth, Bud Angle led off with a walk. The next batter, attempting to sacrifice, forced Bud at second. With the tie breaking run on first and with one out, the batter hit a hard, ground ball to third which was bobbled for an error. Brent was up next. He took off his jacket and walked slowly to the plate. As he stepped into the batter's box, he thought of his close friend, Randy Wood, and the influence the team's captain had had on his life as well as on the lives of other team members.

"Come on, Brent. Hit one out of the park!" called someone from the bench. "Do it for our Preacher boy."

Brent carefully dug a place in which to anchor his right foot.

"Come on, Brent," he whispered to himself. "Get a hit for Randy."

The first pitch was a high slider for a ball. Brent was tempted to swing at the second serve which nipped the outside corner of the plate for a strike. He stepped out of the batter's box and rubbed some dirt on his hands. The next pitch was a fast ball, belt high. Brent watched the ball until it made contact with the bat. The horsehide went over the third baseman's head like a rocket, landing in fair territory by inches. By the time the ball was relayed back to the infield, two runs had scored, and Brent stood on third base with a triple. He scored a moment later on a long sacrifice fly, making the score five to two over the Butler Bull Dogs. The next man grounded out, and the Bull Dogs went into the top of the ninth with the three outs between them and defeat.

Once again, Brent called upon all the strength he could muster in his right arm. The ball popped loudly, pitch after pitch, as it found its target. The opposing batters were no match for the blinding fast ball. Brent threw a called third strike past the last batter, ending the game. Immediately his teammates rushed onto the field, lifted Brent to their shoulders and cheered. The new hero felt as though he would burst with excitement as he was carried off the playing field.

That night, Brent went to Randy's house. "You must have been praying, Randy. I never felt so strong as I did out there today."

"I was praying, Brent. I asked the Lord to help the best team win and . . . I was praying for you, too."

"That's strange," responded Brent. "While I stood at the plate that last time up, I decided to come and talk to you about God and about becoming a Christian. I want to become a Christian, Randy. Your life has really meant something to me."

In a moment the two friends bowed their heads as Brent

confessed his sins and asked Christ to be his Savior. After Randy prayed, they talked about Jim Green.

"Maybe you and I should see Jim," suggested Brent. "After all, he only acts that way because he's not a Christian."

"You're right, Brent. Jim's not a Christian . . . he needs to know Christ, too."

Brent stood up. "If you're up to it, Randy, let's go over to Jim's house tonight. I've got something very special I want to share with him."

"Thank You, Lord," Randy prayed silently. "All things do work together for good to those who love You."

18

WHAT SHALL IT PROFIT?

V. BEN KENDRICK

I don't ever want to see that thing in this room again! Either keep it in your room, or it goes in the garbage!" Henry Miles hovered like a giant over his teenage daughter with his 6'6" frame.

Polly picked up her Bible from the end table where she had laid it. She had just entered the house when her baby brother fell off the front porch. Without stopping to think, she had put her Bible on the table to run and help him. Now, fighting back the tears, she started up the steps to her room.

"I'm sorry, Dad. When I heard Steven cry, I put my Bible on the table without thinking."

"Well, think from now on, and don't let it happen again! What would our friends think if they came in here and saw a Bible? Why, I'd be embarrassed, to say the least."

"Embarrassed isn't even the word for it, Henry," interrupted Polly's mother. "It's bad enough to have our daughter on a religious kick, let alone *insulting* our friends by having her Bible out in the open like we're advertising it."

Polly slipped into her room and knelt beside her bed. It was hard for her to keep back the tears. "Lord," she prayed, "help me to be a good testimony before my family. Dear Father, please save my mom and dad. I love them so very much." She picked up her Bible from the bed and squeezed it tightly. "Thank You, Lord, for Your holy Word."

That evening at the dinner table, Henry Miles told his family of the picnic he was putting on for the mill employees and their families. "I've contracted that new rock group in the city to come play for us. We'll really have a time, with fun and food for everyone." He paused to sip from his glass of beer. "In the morning, we'll have a rip-roaring softball game, and then, after lunch, we have a number of other games lined up, including a horse-shoe-pitching-contest." He glanced at his wife and smiled. "And at night, Dear, we'll have our annual dance."

"When is it, Dad?" Polly asked fearfully.

"It'll be two weeks from this Sunday," answered her father. He then looked at his daughter. "It won't hurt you to give up church this one time."

"But Dad, do I have—"

"Of course you have to go with us. I allow you to go to church, don't I? We're all going, Polly, and that includes you!"

That night, in her room, Polly read her Bible and prayed. She could not help thinking of the conversation which had taken place at the dinner table. The thought of the picnic made her feel ill.

"I can't go," she whispered to herself. "There won't be another Christian there. And besides, there will be drinking and dancing." She knelt by her bed for some time before she began to pray. "Lord, I love You, and I don't want to do anything to dishonor You. Please help me so I won't have to go to the picnic. And Father, please help my parents understand, too."

It was past midnight when Polly awoke to find she was still kneeling beside her bed. As she stood up, she felt deep down inside that somehow God was going to answer her prayer.

Visitors were many in the Miles' home for the next ten days. Factory personnel came and went with only one thought in mind—the annual picnic. Polly overheard her father tell her mother that he had already spent $2,500 for the food and drinks. Nothing was more important than the good time planned for

Sunday. Everything else was secondary in the minds of those planning the big event.

Thursday morning brought with it the makings of a storm. The sky looked threatening with billowing black clouds which seemed to await a signal to unloose their contents on the helpless city below. The weather bureau issued bulletins for heavy rains and high winds. Downtown, inside the Miles' Hosiery Mill, priority number one was the picnic. Already a spirit of festivity was in the air as the announcement was made that there would be no work on Friday in order to give time for the final preparations for the big day. Outside, drops of rain began to fall.

Henry Miles had just entered the mill's parking lot when it happened. The bolt of lightning struck the back part of the building, sending forth a burst of flames. It struck a supply of highly flammable chemicals which began a series of explosions, spewing fire over the other parts of the mill.

"Get out! Leave the building!" shouted the owner as he ran to the front door. There he was met by a flood of workers scrambling for their lives.

"Jim Reese was hurt, Mr. Miles," called one of the workers. "Some of the men carried him out the side door."

Panic reigned as men and women tried to pour through the door opening. Within minutes, the familiar sirens and honking of the fire engines could be heard approaching. The entire building appeared to be made of cardboard as it became engulfed in one big flame.

"It's gone. It's all gone," spoke a dazed Henry Miles, watching the destruction from a block away.

The fire burned out of control. Other fire-fighting units from nearby towns were summoned, but were of no help. The building and its contents were a total loss within the hour. Word quickly spread that the annual picnic would be postponed until further notice.

That night in the Miles' home, the air of festivity had disappeared. Henry Miles sat in the front room, a defeated man. Polly silently entered the room and put her arm around her father.

"Are you all right, Dad? Is there something I can do for you?"

"No, thank you, Honey. I'll be OK in a day or so." He hesitated a moment and looked up at his daughter. "Yes, Polly, there is something you can do for me."

The pleasant tone of her father's voice surprised Polly. There seemed to be a different attitude toward her.

"Honey, I've been doing a lot of thinking since the fire this morning. Everything we had was invested in the mill. Yesterday we had it and today it's gone. It's all gone, Polly."

The young Christian stood listening to her father. Never before had he talked to her like that. It seemed as though he was sharing his heart's burden with her. Polly's own heart ached for him and she wished that somehow she could help him.

"Honey," he said, taking her hand, "is there something in the Bible that can help me through this whole mess? Can you read me something, Polly, that will bring me some kind of an answer?"

Excitement gripped Polly's heart. "Oh, yes, Dad, I can. I'll be right back." Polly hurried up the stairs to get her Bible. "Thank You, Lord," she whispered to herself. "There's no picnic, and now dad has asked me to read Your Word to him."

Quickly she picked up her Bible and hurried back down the stairs. The change was unbelievable. Just ten days before she was told that her Bible would be thrown into the garbage if it was found anywhere other than in her room. Now she had been asked to read it to her father. When she entered the room she found that her mother had joined her father.

"I've asked your mother to listen, too, Polly. The Bible is for all of us, isn't it?"

"Yes, it is, Dad. God's Word is for everyone"

Polly prayed inwardly as she opened her Bible. A verse seemed to jump out at her. It was underlined and she knew it by heart. Taking a deep breath, she began to read. " 'For what shall it profit a man, if he shall gain the whole world, and lose his own soul?' "

104

"Does that mean what I think it does, Polly?" interrupted her father.

"What do you mean, Dad?" responded the surprised daughter.

"Well, uh—what I mean is . . . does that refer to wealth?"

"That could be part of it, Dad. The next verse reads, 'Or what shall a man give in exchange for his soul?' "

Henry Miles stroked his chin. His voice shook as he spoke. "That really hits home, Honey. I can see your mother and me in what you've read. Wouldn't you say so, Mary?"

"I think it's all nonsense, Henry," responded Polly's mother. "What has the Bible got to do with the mill fire?"

"It may have plenty to do with it."

Looking at his daughter, the broken man's eyes pleaded for help. "Honey, would you say a prayer for us?"

Her father's request took Polly by surprise. "I would like to pray for you both, Dad."

Reluctantly, Mary Miles got on her knees beside her husband. When Polly finished praying, her father repeated 'amen' after her.

"Thank you, Honey. I feel much better already. I'm sure we're going to have more Bible readings and prayers around here from now on."

Later on in her room, Polly was filled with excitement at what had taken place that evening. "Thank You, Father, for answering prayer. Thank You for the opportunity to read Your Word and pray with mom and dad tonight."

As she dozed off to sleep, a peaceful look was on Polly's face. She knew God was working in her parents' hearts.

19

THE 'NOISEMAKER'

V. BEN KENRICK

Marge looked out the window. "There's a bicycle light out in the drive, Pete. I wonder if one of our Christians is sick."

Even before Marge finished her sentence, Pete Wall was on his feet, heading toward the door. As he stepped outside he heard a familiar voice.

"Hello, Mr. Wall."

"Why, hello, Timothy. What brings you here this time of night? Is there anything wrong?"

The two men shook hands and the African pastor stepped inside the little mission house. "I came to tell you about my uncle Sala. He's the one we were speaking about Wednesday on our way home from the radio station."

"What about him, Timothy?" asked Pete.

"Well, both my uncle and aunt arrived by bus today. Uncle is sick. They have been on the road for two days."

"I remember seeing the bus coming into the city as I was on my way home today," mentioned Pete.

"The doctor at Bangassou gave Uncle Sala a note to give to the doctor here in the city hospital. I put him in the hospital late this afternoon. I talked to the doctor and he says that my uncle is suffering from bilharze. There is a new miracle drug out which they say can possibly save his life."

Pete knew the results of the dreaded disease. It was the biggest killer in the Central African Republic.

"I've come to ask you and Mrs. Wall to pray for Uncle. He has no time for God."

We'll pray for him, Timothy. Please keep us informed of his progress."

"I sure will, Mr. Wall. I'll also tell my aunt that you are praying for Uncle. She'll be glad to hear that."

Saturday morning, Timothy was up bright and early to get some necessary weeding done in his garden. It was nearly 10 o'clock by the time he arrived at the hospital. He had stopped on the way and purchased a radio for Uncle with some of his savings.

"Hello, Uncle," Timothy smiled as he walked into the dimly lit hospital room, "how are you feeling today?"

"I want you to get me out of this place," responded Uncle in anger. "They've done nothing but stick me with needles ever since I've been here. They don't even let me alone at night so I can sleep."

"I can tell you're feeling better," laughed Timothy, holding out the radio. "Here's something I bought for you on my way over."

"I don't want a 'noise maker'," growled Uncle, "Take it back home with you. Besides, " said the old man hesitantly, "You just want me to listen to that religious talk of yours."

Uncle was referring to the radio broadcast that Timothy did each week with Pete Wall. He was often tempted to listen to his nephew on Sunday morning back home in Bangassou. Not that he was interested in what the young pastor said, but there was a certain pride in having a family member talk on the radio. Some of his neighbors even begged him to listen to their radios, but Uncle always refused.

"I'll leave it here on the table, Uncle Sala," spoke Timothy. "All you have to do is turn this knob." Unknown to Uncle, the radio was already tuned to the local station where Pete and Timothy had their broadcast.

That evening, Timothy passed by the mission station to give

107

a report on Uncle to his missionary friends. "I'm sure anxious to see what Uncle does with his radio tomorrow when our program is on the air. My aunt was at the hospital this afternoon, and Uncle had not even touched his radio up to that time."

"Well," answered Pete, "maybe his curiosity will get the best of him yet. Hey, Timothy," spoke the middle-aged missionary with a sound of excitement in his voice. "Do you think your uncle would mind a visit from us tonight?"

"I don't think so, Mr. Wall," responded the pastor.

"Could I pick you up about seven?" asked Pete.

"OK with me," answered Timothy. "I'll be waiting for you."

As Timothy bicycled home after his conversation with Pete, he thought of their taped radio program which would be broadcast the next morning. He recalled the past Wednesday morning when he and Pete made the recording at the government-owned radio station.

The studio warning light had gone out indicating they were no longer on the air. Pete leaned back in the chair, running his fingers through his thinning hair. Timothy closed the radio program folder and put it in his briefcase.

"Well, that's another program, Mr. Wall. Just think," he continued, "on Sunday morning the entire Central African Republic will be listening to us preach the Word of God."

Pete bent over to pick up his briefcase. "That's right, Timothy. With this station representing the official voice of the government, the people wouldn't think of having their radios sit idle."

"And too," added Timothy, "the entire radio time is given to us by the government. We couldn't ask for anything better. You know something, Mr. Wall," continued the African pastor, "all the time I was speaking today, I was thinking about someone very special to me."

Who was it, Timothy?"

"Well, I couldn't help but think of my Uncle Sala who is unsaved. My aunt, who is a Christian, wrote and told me that their neighbors plan to ask my aunt and uncle over for coffee this

108

Sunday morning as well as to hear the broadcast. I'm sure Uncle won't go because he's an enemy to the gospel."

TOOT! TOOT! "Hey, man, get over and let me by," shouted the angry taxi driver. Timothy quickly returned to reality and pedalled to the side of the narrow road.

"I'm sure God put Uncle in the hospital here," the young man spoke aloud, "and His timing is perfect. Uncle Sala won't be in Bangassou to listen to our radio program, but it doesn't mean he won't hear it!" Excitement stirred in Timothy's heart, and his feet seemed to spin as he rode to his home.

Later that evening Pete and Timothy drove over to the hospital. "He's on the second floor, Mr. Wall. Uncle knows all about you. He'll be glad to see you."

Pete was a bit surprised when he saw Uncle Sala. He pictured him a big man and not the short, thin, feeble man who lay on the hospital bed. He reached his hand out to shake that of the old man.

"Thank you, Sir," said the frail African, "for your kindness to our Timothy. He has told us a lot about you."

The visit was a pleasant one as they talked about a number of things. Finally Pete got up to leave. "Sir, do you mind if I pray for you before I leave?"

The old man became furious. "You'll not do that in this room!" he called out in anger. "Leave me alone! Get out of my room!"

Pete was at a loss for words. He could hardly believe that it was the same man. He reached out his hand for the usual handshake only to have it pushed away. He quietly left the room and made his way down the steps. Timothy caught up with him on the ground level.

"Don't think anything about it, Mr. Wall. That's the way he treats me, when I mention the Lord to him."

"Timothy, I think God is working in that man's heart. His words told me to go, but the look in his eyes bespoke fear—maybe fear of death. Your uncle is resisting, but our God is mighty. That old man may give in and listen to the broadcast and we must be there, right outside his room tomorrow morning."

"Why are you going to do that, Pete?" asked Marge, looking somewhat puzzled at her husband when he had told her of his plan to return to the hospital in the morning.

"Because I think that Uncle Sala will be ready to talk about the Lord after he hears Timothy preach that message."

The sun was already rather high in the sky as Pete and Timothy made their way quietly down the corridor of the hospital. They timed their arrival perfectly as they heard their opening remarks on the broadcast. Timothy smiled to himself as he heard Uncle Sala's radio at full volume. The entire second floor could hear it blasting forth its sounds. Pete thought once that he heard Uncle Sala try to join in the singing. He peeked around the door to find the old man lost completely in the program, listening to every word. Finally, Timothy read the Bible and began to preach.

"That's right, Timothy," they could hear Uncle say to himself. "You're right, my son," he continued.

Pete could hardly believe that he was listening to the same man who had chased him from his room the night before. The closing hymn was sung and the invitation given. Timothy thought he heard a sob. He looked into the room and saw Uncle Sala with his face buried in his hands. "God," he cried, "Help me. Oh, help me."

The two men entered the room and knelt beside the bed. Timothy took his uncle's hand. "Uncle Sala, I've come to pray with you. I've come to help you accept Jesus as your Savior."

The thin, feeble arm reached out and a hand rested on Timothy's shoulder. "Thank you, my son. Thank you."

Within minutes the old man and his nephew bowed their heads as Uncle Sala confessed his sins and asked Christ to save him. Timothy then prayed, thanking God for His new babe in Christ. As they finished praying, they both looked at each other and then at the surprised visitor standing in the doorway. Tears of joy filled her eyes.

"Praise the Lord!" cried Uncle's wife, Tessi. "I heard every word of that wonderful prayer. Now we are all one in Christ."

"Now we are all one in Christ," repeated the old man.

110

20

AN ADOPTED GRANDFATHER

V. Ben Kenrick

Sam Hartman had been walking the streets of Manila since early morning, seemingly in a dream world. Discontentment had been brewing in his heart for several months. His questions seemed to go unanswered, and he felt life had no real meaning.

The sound of a familiar hymn caused Sam to stop on the busy sidewalk and listen. His thoughts sped across the many miles to his wife, Helen, and his home in New Zealand. The middle-aged man entered the little church building.

"Mommy! Look! There's Grandpa!" whispered Elizabeth Wren to her mother.

Betty Wren's eyes quickly followed in the direction her five-year-old daughter was pointing. There, making his way down the center aisle of the auditorium was a tall, gray-haired gentleman.

This had not been the first time Elizabeth or her four-year-old brother Danny had referred to people with gray hair as Grandpa or Grandma. Ever since the little family had left Dave's parents in Indianapolis to return to the Philippiines, the two children spoke daily of Grandpa and Grandma Wren.

Unknown to Sam, the singing he had heard was the final

hymn. David Wren closed in prayer and quickly made his way over to the older gentleman. Danny, too, headed for the visitor, and before anyone realized what had happened, he was sitting in the newcomer's lap.

"Grandpa," he said over and over again, looking up into the kind face.

Sam hugged the little golden-haired boy. "What's your name?" he asked, running his fingers through the boy's hair.

"Danny Wren," responded the child.

"I'm sorry," spoke Betty, appearing on the scene. She reached down to pick up her son. "You remind him of his grandfather. He got away from me before I realized what he was thinking."

"Oh, that's all right," answered Sam, "I love children." His eyes reflected sadness as he spoke.

"Hello," said David, reaching out to shake Sam's hand. "Welcome to our service. I'm Dave Wren and this is my wife, Betty. It looks like you've already met Danny. This is Elizabeth."

"Can Grandpa come home with us, Daddy?" asked Elizabeth, looking up pleadingly with her big, blue eyes.

"That all depends on our friend, Honey," replied her father.

"By the way," spoke the latecomer, "my name is Sam Hartman. I'm a seaman on a tanker. We came into port last night. Since the captain gave us time off today, I thought I would walk around town a bit. I recognized the hymn you people were singing and decided I'd go to church this morning. It looks like I got here too late."

"That's all right, Mr. Hartman," said Dave. "If you don't have any plans for dinner, we'd love to have you come home with us."

"It would be a real treat for the children, too," added Betty.

"Well, to tell the truth," said Sam, smiling, "I really don't have any plans. I'd be happy to accept your invitation."

The two children clapped their hands when they heard Sam's response to their parents' invitation. "Mommy," asked Elizabeth excitedly, "may I sit by Grandpa at the table?"

"Honey, you both may sit by Mr. Hartman," answered her

mother. As Betty spoke, she looked toward Sam. For a moment she thought she saw tears in his eyes.

The little family, with their new friend, made their way to the light blue Toyota parked nearby. As the car wound its way through the crowded streets, Sam shared a bit more about himself. Dave and Betty were surprised to hear that Sam was from New Zealand and not the United States as they had assumed. Elizabeth and Danny sat quietly beside their newfound friend as the older folks talked together. Several times Dave attempted to direct the conversation to spiritual matters, but each time he was unsuccessful. The missionary felt Sam didn't want to discuss such matters in front of the children.

"Here we are," said Dave, as he pulled into the white gravel driveway and parked the car beside an attractive cottage.

Betty went inside with the children while Dave showed Sam around the yard.

Before long the Wren family and their visitor sat down to eat. Dave prayed and thanked the Lord for the food. A chill ran up Sam's spine as the missionary prayed for him, too.

"Thank You, Father, for directing Sam to us today. We're happy to have him as our guest. Watch over his family wherever they are today. Minister to their hearts according to their needs. In Jesus' name. Amen."

As they ate, Sam looked across the table at Betty. "The food is delicious, Betty. My wife prepares her meatloaf just like this."

Again, a note of sadness could be detected in Sam's voice.

After dinner, the children listened while Sam told them stories of life on the high seas and then went to bed for their afternoon nap. Sam and Dave sat and talked as Betty cleared the table and worked in the kitchen.

"Tell me more about your family, Sam. How many children do you have?"

"I have two boys and a girl. All three are married now. My daughter, the youngest, was just married three months ago. I was able to make it home for the wedding."

"That's great," responded Dave, wondering how to approach Sam about spiritual matters. "Tell me about your wife. Does she mind your being away for long periods of time?"

"I'm sure she does, although she doesn't say much about it. I have one more year to go, and then I can retire. We're both looking forward to that. I have a wonderful wife, Dave."

Sam struggled to hold back the tears as he spoke. "I couldn't help but think of her as I stood out on the street today, listening to the singing."

"What do you mean, Sam?" questioned Dave.

"She believes like you folks. My wife is a Christian."

The seaman's answer took Dave by surprise. Just then Betty returned to the room to join the men.

"Honey, did you hear what Sam just told me? His wife's a Christian."

"That's wonderful, Sam," replied Betty. "It must make you feel good to know that wherever you go in the world, you have a wife praying for your safety."

"It does, Betty," said Sam, looking sadly at the floor. "She's praying that I'll get saved, too. I know it's because of her prayers that I'm here with you today. Just wait until I write and tell her."

"Sam," said Dave in a serious tone, "wouldn't it be great news if the letter told of your salvation?"

The room became silent. Dave waited for Sam to answer. Betty sat with her head slightly bowed, praying for their new friend. Both Dave and Betty sensed that Sam was carrying a great burden.

The sad-faced seaman gave a big sigh and then said, "Shortly after Helen and I were married, she became a Christian. She prayed faithfully for me that we would be one in Christ. Just a few years ago, I began to think that maybe she did have something I wanted. Maybe God was the answer. I decided to give it more thought, but not just then."

Sam stopped for a moment to gain control of his emotions. "About the same time, our first grandchild came along. She was our pride and joy. Her name was Penny, and she had the most beautiful blond hair you ever saw. When Penny was two, she was struck by a car and died several hours later. I can't begin to

114

describe our grief. I blamed God for Penny's death. Helen's attitude toward God never changed, but I became bitter. Helen still lived for Him and spoke of her love for Him. Knowing she loved Him made me even more angry. I couldn't understand how she could love God when He allowed our Penny to be taken from her parents and us."

A tear trickled from Sam's eye. Another followed. "But Helen's faithful Christian life began to soften my hardened heart. This morning I realized I had come to the end of myself and that's why I came into your service. When your dear children mistook me for their grandpa, I felt that God was reaching me through them. I know I can't continue this way. Helen has been so patient with me in my bitterness and unbelief. I feel so lonesome at times, knowing that she and the children are Christians. Dave, I want to be saved."

Without saying another word, Sam slipped to his knees and began to sob. "Oh, God, I need You. I've tried to run from You for so many years and I'm tired of running. Forgive me of my sins, and make me Your child today. God, please save me."

Dave and Betty knelt beside Sam. When Sam finished praying, Dave prayed, thanking God for directing Sam to them and for saving him.

"Is it possible to send a cable today?" asked Sam, standing to his feet and wiping his eyes. "I'd love to send this good news to Helen right away."

"The telegraph office is open until four o'clock," answered Dave. "I'll take you now if you wish."

Within an hour the cable was on its way to New Zealand, telling a faithful prayer warrior that her prayers had been answered, and she was now one in Christ with her husband.

Betty and the children met the men as they entered the front door.

"The children asked where you were, Sam," Betty said with a sparkle in her eyes. "I told them their 'grandpa' has something he wants to tell them."

"With pleasure," said Sam, picking up both children. "Today I think I'm the happiest grandpa in the whole world!"

21

NIGHT PROWLER

NINA KENDRICK

The chapel was buzzing that rainy season morning as Ann made her way down the dirt road in the chill mist. The women's class was held very early this time of year so they could still work in their gardens for several hours before the heat drove them back to the village or to the shelter of a shade tree. Ann could hear the chatter long before she reached the mud brick, thatch roofed building. Usually the women were very subdued at this hour and talked quietly among themselves. She knew that something had happened. Hurrying down the aisle, the young missionary walked between the brick and cement benches and was greeted on either side by voices shrill with excitement.

"Mamma, did you hear . . . ?"

"We were so frightened!"

"We didn't know what it was."

Getting these ladies quieted down enough to find out what the trouble was, was no easy task. Their eyes were still round with fright, and many of their faces were covered with perspiration in spite of the cold.

"What has happened to make you all so afraid?" Ann finally managed to wedge her question in between their agitated talk.

"Why, Mamma," the self-appointed spokeswoman began,

"When Louise and I came into God's house this morning, we saw something move in the shadows up front. We jumped back to the side of the door, and a huge leopard rushed past us. He used God's house for his sleeping last night!"

A leopard! The missionaries knew they were in the neighborhood. Many nights they had heard the peculiar grunt near the house, but the possibility of encountering one face-to-face had never occured to Ann. She was glad she hadn't been the first one to arrive that morning. It was better not to let anyone know how scared she was. With a couple of fast songs, the class was started and the spotted visitor forgotten for the time being.

Later in the week, the Foster household was awakened by voices in the backyard. Dressing quickly, Ann and Bryan, her husband, went outside to see what was happening. The workmen were clustered around the miniature hut that served as a goat house. One was pointing excitedly to a place on the roof. Going closer, the young couple could see what looked like long scratches where patches of grass had been clawed off. They soon realized that friend leopard had paid another visit. The night prowler was getting pretty close to home!

Several days passed. There are always many jobs for a missionary to do. Everyone was busy, and the leopard incidents slipped gradually to the back of their minds. Perhaps, deep in their consciousness was the hope that *he* had forgotten *them*. Whatever the reason, the oversized tabby was just now making himself scarce.

Early one morning, Ann and Bryan heard clapping hands outside their door. (An African never knocks. If he wishes to see you, he either claps his hands or he coughs.) This morning they could tell by the intensity of Luke's clapping that he was very eager to make his presence known. Hastily they opened the door.

"Mister," Luke cried, "Go and look at the back entrance!" Hurrying to the other side of the house, they entered the bedroom of their little daughter, for this was where the back door was located. The door, covered only with screen wire, had a large indentation which hadn't been there the night before.

Arriving at the mission station that morning, the workmen began, as usual, to look around to see that everything was in order. Near the back of the house they spied tracks which they immediately recognized as those of the leopard. Following the tracks they realized with dismay that they led right to this back door. Trying to gain entrance to the house, the animal had pressed his head into the screen. Penny, the Foster's three-year-old daughter, lay sleeping in this room! Psalm thirty-four, verse seven sprang simultaneously to their lips: "The angel of the Lord encampeth round about those who fear Him, and delivereth them." Here was one more evidence of God's loving care for them.

Now, something had to be done about this unwelcome wanderer. This latest happening was just too close for comfort. With the help of the workmen, Bryan proceeded to rig a gun trap. This contraption involves two compartments, one of which houses a small animal . . . in this case a goat. The leopard, scenting the animal, walks through a passage over which is poised a shotgun. Striking a string which is fastened to the trigger, the hunted one becomes his own executioner.

It was Wednesday night and the little band of missionaries gathered for prayer. After prayer meeting the two single ladies, one a nurse, the other a teacher, stepped out on the back porch preparing to go back to their tiny house across the station. As a precaution, Bryan went to the edge of the verandah and flashed his light around the yard.

"Get back into the house," he whispered. "I see the eyes of the leopard."

The girls laughed. "Oh, you are always trying to scare us. We knew before we came tonight that you would try that one on us!"

"Look, then," he hissed. In the flashlight beam they could see the unmistakeable emerald green eyes flash. One can always tell a leopard by the green eyes. Had this been a lion, the light would have picked up a red gleam. No one needed to be told twice. It was a contest to see who could get through the door first. The four of them stood in the living room waiting. Within minutes, the boom of the shotgun reverberated through the still night. Shivers of dread raced through them. Was he dead? Maybe he was just wounded and more dangerous than ever. Perhaps he got away without a scratch. This sometimes happened. All these thoughts cascaded through their thoughts as they stood frozen.

Bryan broke the spell by picking up his large gun and heading for the door. After rigging the trap that afternoon he had taken the advice of Luke, the head workman, and had parked the pick-up close to the porch steps. Now it was an easy jump to the cab.

As soon as they heard the report of the gun, three of the workmen returned to the mission station. Ever since it had become dark they had been listening for that sound as they sat around their little fires with their families in front of their huts. Knowing how vicious an injured cat can be, they came to help 'Mister'. Two of them climbed into the truck bed just as Bryan started the motor. Luke climbed into the cab beside him. How thankful he was to have these faithful friends with him.

Reaching the trap site, they could see the leopard lying partway into the tunnel-like structure. There was no motion but, rather than assume that he was dead, Bryan cautiously opened the door and poked carefully at the animal with the butt of his gun. Having made certain that there was no life remaining, the four men picked up the carcass and put it into the back of the pick-up. The little goat, still trembling with fright, was released from his small prison and returned to the goat house.

Ann and the other ladies gathered eagerly around the truck to see the prize as it was unloaded. Calling for a tape measure, Bryan found that the magnificent beast was just two inches short of eight feet from the tip of his nose to the tip of his tail. What a stunning rug he would make! Bryan would have the hide cured with salt by an African who, he knew, would do an excellent job. When they went home on furlough next year, he would take it to an expert and have it made into a cherished rug. This would be a constant reminder to the Foster family that God was always watching over them.

One of Ann and Bryan's favorite verses had new meaning to them now, and even Penny could recite it without a flaw in her soft little voice.

"Fear thou not; for I am with thee: Be not dismayed; for I am thy God: I will strengthen thee; yea, I will uphold thee with the right hand of my righteousness" (Isa. 41:10).

The Heavenly Father had sent the Fosters to this needy land to win lost ones to Himself. He didn't expect them to go alone, and armed with His promises, they were doing the job He had called them to do. The leopard incident was just one of many that was being woven into a beautiful pattern of service for the Master.

"O taste and see that the LORD is good: blessed is the man that trusteth in Him" (Ps. 34:8).

22

OUT OF THE LION'S MOUTH

V. BEN KENDRICK

Kadja lifted the last steaming sweet potato from the large, black pot. Only a few red coals remained underneath the well-used cooking vessel. Carefully, she placed the potato with the others on a large, flat board which served as her work counter. Her nimble fingers worked expertly as she peeled off the skins. The smell of the potatoes caused Mamela to look up from the chaise lounge where he was relaxing.

"Those potatoes seem to smell extra good tonight, Kadja," remarked her farmer-husband.

"It is only because you are extra hungry," answered the smiling, middle-aged African woman. "After all, you have not had any food since your coffee and biscuit this morning."

It was not unusual for an African to go from morning to evening without eating. They always looked forward to the evening meal which was the large meal of the day. It was the custom for the father and sons to eat first, and what was left would then be given to the mother and daughters. Since Mamela and Kadja never had children, they always ate at the same time.

After she finished peeling the potatoes, Kadja picked up the cooking pot and made her way toward the back of the hut.

Village law forbade anyone to throw cooking or wash water in front of any of the huts. The moonless sky made it difficult for her to see where she was walking. She carefully knelt down and placed the hot pot of water on the ground. Just as she began tipping it over, she felt a painful vise-like grip on her head. Her horrified scream sent Mamela tumbling out of his chaise lounge. He raced to the back of the hut but was not able to see anything in the darkness.

"Kadja! Where are you? What is wrong?"

A deep, low growl told the African that he was right next to a lion. Fear gripped him but the thought of his wife caused him to plunge headlong into the darkness toward the sound of the wild beast.

"Kadja!" he called again, "Do you hear me?"

Fear gave way to anger as Mamela flayed out with his hands hoping to get hold of the attacking animal. He heard the low growl again but this time, farther away. Without warning, his feet hit something on the ground and sent him sprawling headlong into the dirt. A nearby groan caused him to bounce right back up.

"Kadja! Is that you?" The concerned husband bent down and found his wife lying on the ground at his feet. "Kadja, speak to me. Say something."

Another groan came from the wounded woman. Just then several villagers appeared carrying torches. Mamela felt sick as he saw the ugly fang marks on Kadja's head. Blood covered her face from the deep bites. Her dress was torn from her back revealing long bloody gashes caused by the lion's claws. The fear-filled husband placed his head close to his wife's face. "Kadja, can you hear me?"

Slowly her eyes opened and her lips began to move. "Yes," she said softly, "I can hear you."

"She is speaking!" called Mamela to the gathering crowd. "She is talking to me!"

Someone appeared with a blanket and pole. "We must take her to the mission station. Mademoiselle will help her."

Kadja was carefully lifted onto the blanket spread on the

122

ground beside her. The ends of the blanket were then tied to the ends of the pole which was immediately lifted to the shoulders of two young men. Within minutes the group of villagers began their twenty mile walk to the mission dispensary.

Roy Kintner had just completed giving his work assignments to the station workmen and turned to go back to the house for breakfast. He stopped suddenly as he saw several people heading for the dispensary. Two of the men were carrying a blanket case between them.

"Tagba!" he called to the head workman. "Run quickly to Mademoiselle's house and tell her a blanket case just arrived at the dispensary."

Within minutes Marge White was on her bicycle, pedalling hard to her emergency case. When she arrived, she found Kadja semi-conscious and in a state of shock. The long night had taken its toll on the African woman. The missionary nurse began to work fervently to gain control of the situation.

"Is she going to die, Mademoiselle?" asked Mamela standing close by and watching the nurse's every movement. "We brought her as fast as we could get here."

"I'm not sure what will happen," replied Marge, silently praying as she worked. "Those bites are deep and infection has already set in. She is in God's hands."

An hour later, the nurse called her dispensary workers together to pray for Kadja. Mamela, along with several others from his village, joined the medical staff. The bush farmer watched as the workers reverently bowed their heads.

"What a strange way to talk to their God," he thought. "I have to cry out to my gods and even make sacrifices and dance for them."

Several of the staff prayed, asking God to spare Kadja's life and that she would come to know and trust Him as her God. Marge was the last one to pray. As Mamela listened to her, he was impressed with the friendly relationship that existed between the missionary nurse and her God. He was pleased to hear her say his name along with Kadja's.

"Dear Father," prayed Marge, "please give me wisdom in

treating Kadja. Heal her, Lord, and may she and Mamela come to know You as their God."

As she finished her prayer, a hum of 'amens' could be heard about the room. Mamela felt within himself that he, too, wanted to know the God the missionary and her workers knew—a God they seemed to know as a close friend.

That afternoon, Kadja showed good improvement. When Marge visited her at four o'clock, she was surprised to see such a big change in her patient.

"My liver thanks you, Mademoiselle, for taking good care of me."

The nurse smiled at Kadja's remark, realizing that the Africans always used the word liver in place of heart in expressing their feelings.

"You are welcome, Kadja," replied Marge. "I'm sure you will be all right now. You arrived just in time. Those bites are very deep."

"I did not see the lion when I went behind the house to empty the cooking water. There was no moonlight at all. When I stooped to dump the water on the ground, the lion took my head into its mouth. I guess my scream scared it because I could have been killed right then."

"It's a miracle that you are alive, Kadja. God spared your life, and He brought you here to the dispensary," said Marge, smiling as she took her patient's blood pressure.

Just then Roy walked into the dispensary with Mamela, whose face was beaming. Kadja turned to look at her husband. She had never seen him so happy.

"I know Him, Kadja! I know the God of the missionaries."

"What do you mean, Mamela?" questioned his wife, somewhat confused by her husband's sudden happiness.

"I heard them pray for us this morning. Just to listen to them made my liver feel good. I decided that I would ask Mr. Kintner to help me know his God. We sat down and he told me all about Jesus Who is God's Son. Jesus died for our sins, Kadja. We do not have to be afraid when we die if we believe in Jesus to take care of us."

124

Kadja turned to look at Marge who quietly explained God's plan of salvation to her. Now and then, Mamela would click his tongue to show his agreement with what the nurse was saying. When she finished, her patient's eyes were filled with tears.

"I want to know Jesus, too," she said in a quiet voice. "If God can do that for Mamela, can He do it for me, too?"

"Yes, He can," said Roy. "He can save you right where you are, Kadja, if you will confess your sins and ask Him to make you His child."

Marge talked further with her patient and then prayed with her. When Kadja asked Jesus to become her Savior, a loud click could be heard all over the room from Mamela's throat. It was his tribal way of showing his happy approval of what was taking place.

"Now, we both know God," said Mamela showing his filed, pointed teeth as he smiled.

"Yes, we do," responded Kadja. "I am glad for all that has happened—even if it meant for God to take me out of the lion's mouth to send me here."

The remark from the happy woman brought laughter from her friends.

23

WHOM THE LORD LOVETH, HE CHASTENETH

V. BEN KENDRICK

Lois Swank slammed the bedroom door and threw herself on her bed. She beat hard on the pillows with her clenched fists.

"Why don't they allow me to live my own life?" she sobbed. "I'm old enough to know what I want!"

It was Lois' seventeenth birthday and Ed Tripp had asked her to go with him to a drive-in-movie. Ed was a tall, good looking high school senior who was the school's basketball star. Lois had often confided to friends that she thought it would be the ultimate to go out with Ed, even though he wasn't a Christian. She had heard some talk of him smuggling beer into the school, but like many other news bits, that could easily have been a rumor. Now, to think Ed had chosen to ask her out of the hundreds of girls in school.

Lois had accurately predicted how her parents would react to her announcement of a date with Ed.

"But you're a Christian, Honey," said her mother. "You know what the Bible says about dating unbelievers."

Lois stared sullenly, then shouted, "What do you think he

is, Mom? A barbarian? He's just as good as anyone in this house. You're prejudiced! That's what you are!"

Her mother's eyes filled with tears. Lois dramatically stamped up the stairs to her room, giving the door a hard slam.

Sam Swank arrived at six o'clock sharp. He noticed his wife's red eyes as soon as he entered the house.

"What's wrong, Martha? Have you been crying?" He quickly went to her side. She reluctantly told him about her conversation with their daughter.

"All I said to her, Sam, was that she was a Christian girl and should not date unsaved boys. She then raced up to her room, crying." Martha looked at her husband. "I've noticed that Lois has not been herself lately. There seems to be something troubling her."

The concerned mother buried her face in her hands. "What's happened, Sam? During these past couple of months, Lois seems to have lost her interest in the things of the Lord. Oh, Sam, I'm worried about her."

That night Lois "disciplined" her wayward parents with the silent treatment. Several times they tried to engage her in conversation but without success. She returned to her room immediately after the meal and stayed there. The next morning she arrived at the breakfast table at seven o'clock, surprising her parents with her early rising.

"I'm leaving home," she announced gaily. "Don't try to stop me. I've made up my mind."

The middle-aged couple were stunned to hear their daughter talk like this.

"I packed my luggage last night. I called Ed and he's picking me up. He'll be here any time now. I've asked him to take me somewhere."

A car horn sounded as Ed Tripp pulled into the drive. Lois' mother reached out to take her daughter by the arm.

"No, Mom! I'm not changing my mind. I know what I'm doing."

Before they could stop her, Lois opened the door and ran to the waiting car. Unknown to her bereaved parents, Ed had picked up the two suitcases that Lois had hidden behind the bushes during the night.

Sam Swank ran to get his car from the garage, but Ed had already disappeared into the traffic with Lois. The Swanks were stunned. Their hearts were crushed. Their only daughter had run away from home.

Sam notified the police, who said they would keep a lookout for Lois. Each hour seemed like an eternity to the distraught parents.

Four days dragged by before the first word came from Lois. It came by way of a telephone call.

"Mom, I just wanted you to know that I've found a job and an apartment. I'm all right, and I don't want you to try to find me."

"But, Honey, can't we even see you?" begged her mother. "Maybe we can arrange to meet you somewhere just to talk things over."

"Not now, Mom," answered Lois, coldly. "I'll call you when I'm ready to see you!"

That night Martha slept very little. Should they call their son, Tom, at Bible college and tell him about his sister? Not wanting to interfere with his exams, they decided to wait until he came home in a few days. They would tell him then.

Two days later, Tom called to say he was leaving for home that afternoon after his last exam. His eagerness to get home meant he would drive all night. Before she drifted off to sleep that night, Martha prayed for her children as usual, committing them to the Lord.

At first she thought she was dreaming; then she realized it was the phone! Sam reached over and picked it up.

"Hello! Yes, this is the Swank residence. Speaking. He what? When did it happen. I see. Thank you for calling."

"Sam, what is it? Sam, is it Lois?" Martha was crying.

Sam, as if in a trance, placed the receiver on the phone and slowly turned to his wife. "Tom had an accident on his way home. He's with the Lord, Martha."

The news of Tom's death left Martha and Sam in a state of

shock. "If Tom weren't living for the Lord, I could understand it," Martha sobbed.

"I know, Honey," her husband said brokenly.

Early the next morning they called the pastor and he came to their home immediately. Arrangements were made for Tom's body to be shipped home. All efforts to contact Lois failed. They were hesitant to set the funeral date, but were finally forced to do so. The days seemed to drag on. At last, Friday, the day of the funeral arrived. Still no word came from Lois. As the grieving parents stood beside the open grave, only the Lord knew the terrible anguish in their hearts. Understanding friends and relatives had to be told about Lois' flight and, therefore, avoided mention of her in conversation.

Few people noticed the taxi that stopped just outside the cemetery. A lone figure emerged, clad in a dark dress, and quickly made her way to join the little gathering at the graveside. Lois' eyes scanned the group and rested on the two people standing silently beside the pastor.

"Mom! Dad!" she cried, racing over to them. Lois threw herself into her mother's arms. "Oh, Mom! Mom!" she sobbed.

Sam Swank reached out and put his arms around his wife and daughter. "Thank the Lord, Honey. God has brought you back home. He has answered our prayers."

"But, Dad," cried Lois.

"It's all right, Honey," comforted her father. "Your brother is with the Lord Whom he loved. Everything is all right. We have you back home."

Sam's face was wet with tears as he spoke. A mixture of sorrow and joy filled his heart.

A short time later, on their way back home, Lois told her parents how she had heard about her brother's death. They sat and listened as she spoke.

"This morning one of the girls in the apartment house read about the funeral in the paper and asked if Tom was a relative. I couldn't believe it when I read that he was killed. Mom, I just stood there and cried."

"Well, Honey," said her father finally, "the Lord never

makes a mistake. He allowed this to happen to Tom for His glory. We must believe that He is good and perfect in all that He does."

There was silence in the car for several moments before Lois responded.

"God took Tom to bring me home. Oh, Mom, I'm so sorry for the terrible things I said to you! I never thought God would take Tom to punish me."

Lois buried her head in her hands and wept softly. "I've asked the Lord to forgive me. Will you forgive me, too? I've been so cruel to both of you."

"Honey," said her father, "the Bible says, 'whom the Lord loveth, He chasteneth.' We do forgive you, Lois. It means so much to have you back home again and to know that you've given the Lord His proper place in your life."

That night Lois and her parents had family devotions together. There was one less member of the family now. "And, Father," she prayed, "if You want me to go to Bible school, I'm willing to go. I want only Your will for my life."

Later that night as Martha lay quietly listening to the sounds of the night, amidst the sorrow of just burying her son, she had perfect peace in her heart—peace in the knowledge that God was in control and that their daughter had returned.

24

IDENTICAL TWINS

NINA KENDRICK

"Are you ready yet, Holly?" Holly could hear the irritation in her dad's voice.

"No wonder," she thought, half aloud. She *had* been dragging her feet; she didn't want to go! Quickly she put the last dish in the cupboard, bathed her hands in soft, pink lotion and dashed them across her skirt to wipe off the excess. Turning off the light, she hurried into the living room.

Mr. Marsch already had his coat on and was standing at the window. His wife, Susan, sat reading by the fireplace. Bright yellow and blue flames cast a soft glow over her delicate features. Holly couldn't help but admire the cozy scene, but upon seeing the white cast on her mother's wrist, Holly's face took on a petulant look. Jed Marsch noted his daughter's expression and spoke softly.

"Honey, I know this is difficult for you. I'm really sorry, but you know Mom can't drive with that broken wrist. Don't worry, you'll do fine. But we must hurry. There is a snow storm headed this way."

Reluctantly Holly pulled on her jacket and boots. Picking up her gloves she started for the door. Suddenly she stopped and crossed to where her mother sat. Bending, she kissed her quickly on the cheek.

"Bye, Mum. See you soon."

Dad had the car warming and it felt good, for even the short walk across the yard to the driveway had been chilling. She observed that the wind had risen and glanced anxiously at the sky. Already black clouds were scudding across the dark heavens. Holly shivered as she slammed the car door.

The fifty miles to the city passed mostly in silence. Jed finally spoke.

"Honey, I really feel unhappy that you have to spend your evening like this, but I have to get the car tonight. I made an appointment for tomorrow morning at the garage for this one. Besides, if we don't get it tonight, there is no telling when we'll be able to with that storm moving in."

"I know, Daddy, but you *know* I have never driven that far alone before. After all, I have only had my license for three weeks. I'll be absolutely petrified!" Her voice rose shrilly.

"You are a good driver, Baby, and I'll be close by most of the way. I do have to stop and see Mr. Andrews, but that leaves only ten miles of the trip remaining after my turn-off. Just drive carefully like you always do. Don't worry!"

"Sure, it's fine for you to talk," Holly grumbled to herself. "I'm always the one who has to give things up. My darling brother never misses his basketball games." Holly knew she was being unreasonable. Greg wasn't even old enough to drive! It just made her so angry that he always got *his* way and she *never* did.

Anger had become a familiar part of her these days. Mom and Dad didn't understand her. She *had* to go to Sunday school. She *had* to go to church all day Sunday and Wednesday nights, too. She *had* to go to Young People's. She could never have any *real* fun like the kids at school did. It was all so boring. Her friends thought her parents were terribly old fashioned. It was so embarrassing!

Holly was unaware that they had arrived at their destination. She had been so deep in her thoughts. Her father's voice broke into her tumult.

132

"Here we are, Honey. I'll go in and get the papers taken care of. Want to come along?"

"I'll wait here, but please hurry. It is starting to snow."

Disappointed at her lack of interest in the new car, Jed hurried into the brightly lighted showroom. By the time he returned, the ground was already white.

The dejected figure, slumped in the seat, made his heart ache. He and Susan had spent many sleepless nights talking about and praying for their beloved daughter. It was hard to understand what had happened to change this child of theirs into such an unhappy person. They remembered the day she had asked the Lord Jesus into her heart and life. She had been such a joyful Christian, taking part in all the activities at church, singing in a gospel trio, even doing hospital visitation. Now, suddenly, she was someone they hardly knew. He shook his head as he opened the door.

"Sure you are awake enough to drive, Kitten?" he teased. Then, rumpling her hair, he tossed her the keys. "You won't have any trouble following me tonight. There probably won't be much traffic. I'll be getting off at Rogers Road, but you go on home. Mom will be anxious. See you a little later."

As Jed predicted, there were very few cars on the road, and Holly began to feel more at ease behind the wheel. Once or twice she felt herself slide and knew the road was becoming icy. She saw her father's turn signal flash for a right-hand turn and knew she had just ten more miles. She was almost home! She wondered why she had been so afraid. This was fun. Without realizing it, her foot pressed lightly on the accelerator, and the car leaped forward.

She was going too fast . . . she drove onto the bridge and hit a slick patch. The frightened girl could feel the car begin to skid and heard herself screaming. When the machine left the road it began to turn over as though in slow motion. Holly felt like she was suspended in time until she felt the bump that told her the auto had landed on its top. Then she experienced a silence so profound that the slight figure could almost feel it surrounding her. Thinking quickly, she reached to turn off the ignition and unfastened her seat belt as she thought aloud in the eerie quietness.

"I never was one for hanging upside down . . . I'll take the upright approach any day." Giggling hysterically, she reached for the door handle. As she gave it a wrench, searing pain shot up her arm. With determination, she fought off the faintness and with her left hand this time, pushed at the door. It was jammed as was the one opposite.

Panic loomed close to the surface. The cold was intense now that the motor was idle. She was glad for her goosedown jacket, but that only covered a limited area. The rest of her was becoming terribly cold. Shivering uncontrollably now, hot tears coursed down her cheeks. Even the burning tears quickly turned to icy fingers and seemed to leave grooves in her flesh. Holly had just recently read an article about freezing to death. Was that to be her fate? Much like a small explosion in her brain, she suddenly remembered the afghan Grandma had put in the back seat the last time they had visited her.

"It might be cold, Holly-kins. Take this with you." She had thrust the bright, fluffy square into her hands. Maybe it was still there. She hadn't even thought about it since that time. Cautiously, on hands and knees, she probed the back seat area. It was easy with the car upside down! Sure enough, in the far corner she felt the softness of Grandma's gift. Gratefully Holly wrapped herself in its warmth and sank back against the side of the vehicle. She knew the newfound warmth was only temporary. The thermometer was dropping, and it was snowing harder now—almost a blizzard. Would anyone ever find her? Would they be in time? She wished she had never read that article!

Susan Marsch pulled the drapes back and watched anxiously as the snow grew deeper in the front yard. Greg had come home from basketball practice and was at the kitchen table wolfing down his warmed-up dinner.

Wandering into the room, his mother put her fears into words. "Greg, it seems that Dad and Holly should be home by now. Holly isn't used to driving distances alone, and this snow really has me worried!"

134

"Ah, Mom, they'll be along. Don't worry. This snow storm has slowed them down. Holly is a good driver, even if she *is* my sister and a woman driver, too!" He grinned at his mom.

A smile cut through the frown on Mrs. Marsch's face. She knew that this was the nearest Greg would come to complimenting his sister, and he would never say it to her face! He would never let anyone know how fond he was of Holly.

"Well, Son, we *can* help them get back safely. Let's ask the Lord to take care of our loved ones." Mother and son bowed their heads and asked their Heavenly Father to watch over the absent ones.

Holly's thoughts were a jumble. Uppermost was the memory of the quick kiss on her mother's cheek and the look of surprised pleasure it had evoked. Shamefully, she realized that she could not recall the last time she had shown her mother any affection. In fact, she hadn't displayed much love for anyone lately. Her main aim and desire was to be just like the kids at school.

Suddenly, incidents started crowding her mind, and none of them made her feel very proud. Her life in recent months was anything but Christ-like. The Lord had been so good to her, giving her not only parents and a brother (who after all was not so bad), but many other things. She had a warm, comfortable, beautiful home. She loved pretty clothes, and her closet was bulging with them. She had never gone hungry, except when an extra pound or two caused her to "crash diet." That never lasted long—Mom was too good a cook. Oh, she groaned, her parents loved her so much, and she had hurt them so terribly. Even Greg made it a point to keep out of her way. Poor Greg, she really had been a mean sister. Would he ever forgive her? Would she ever see him again?

Her thoughts turned to the snug living room, her soft bed, the well-stocked cookie jar. She was so hungry. Oddly enough, she thought of the little red brick church which she and her family had attended as long as she could remember. Lately she had argued with her parents every time there was a service. Now she longed to hear the organ play, to be with the girls in her Sunday school class; she had called them "holier-than-thou," and her cheeks again burned with shame. Maybe they wouldn't care if she never came back . . . if she died! How could she blame them? She wanted to hear Pastor Edwards preach again. Rebelliously, she had created many disturbances during the most solemn part of the observances. Just last Sunday she had let a songbook fall from the balcony, and it had narrowly missed Mrs. Olding, who sat below. In spite of Holly's rude behavior, the Pastor was always kind to her and radiated the love of Christ. She suddenly realized that she didn't want to lose any of the good things she had, and tears began to rain down her face.

Perhaps they wouldn't find her in time, and she would die here all alone. No, she wasn't alone. She hadn't been living for Jesus lately, but He had said in Hebrews 13:5, "I will never leave thee, nor forsake thee." If she died tonight, she knew she would go to be with Him. But, oh, she didn't want to meet Him as she was now; she had many things to make right first.

"Dear Father, I know You are with me right now. You will never leave me alone. Please forgive me for ignoring You for such a long time. Forgive me, please, for hurting my parents and Greg. I've cheated in school, and I've lied to Mom and Dad. If You do allow me to be found, help me to live for You and to make right all the wrong things I have done. Most of my friends at school don't even know I'm a Christian, Lord. Help me to live a Christian life and to tell them about You. I've never told any of them, Lord, and I want to be a good witness and to live a clear testimony for You. And dear Jesus, if it can please You, please help them to find me soon!" In spite of the intense pain in her arm, Holly began to doze.

"Help them to find me soon . . . help them to find me soon . . . help them. . . ." The words hung on the frosty air. Holly could hear herself as she drifted in and out of consciousness. How cold she felt! Even the goosedown jacket and the afghan had lost their effectiveness, and her arm hurt so. Misery engulfed her. Struggling as though through a thick fog, Holly could hear faint voices.

"I wonder who is outside so late at night," she murmured dreamily. A loud knock on the windshield woke her up.

136

"Holly, Holly honey, are you in there? Are you all right?" Tugging fruitlessly at the blocked door, Holly's father called, "Hang in there, Sweetie, we'll get you out." Holly could hear the anguish in her father's voice, but the huge lump in her throat prevented a reply. Warmth enveloped her while outside she could hear the sound of frenzied activity. Soon the door was pried open and gentle hands were lifting her out. Her father crushed her in a bear hug.

"Oh, Daddy, I didn't think you would ever find me. It was so cold and so dark and my arm hurts so much!" Holly felt like a tiny girl again as her father tenderly maneuvered her to the new car. A policeman motioned him to follow his black and white vehicle. The flashing red light served as a beacon to lead them through the swirling snow.

Father and daughter had much to discuss. Holly was heartbroken over the wrecked car, but Jed Marsch was too thankful at having his daughter safe and sound to even bother about a banged up auto. He recounted that upon arriving home and realizing that Holly was missing, he had set out with police aid to retrace the route home. Surely God had directed the search, for the thick snow had quickly obliterated all trace of her skid. Remembering that only a week before a car had gone off that same bridge, the police had started their search there.

Fear and joy mingled as the car was dug from the mound of fresh snow. Jed's voice broke when he told Holly how he rejoiced upon finding her alive. With the pain in her arm nearly forgotton, Holly was surprised when they drew up to the door of the emergency ward.

"We'll have a doctor look you over, but first let's call your mother. She's been waiting a long time!"

After the physician had set her fractured wrist and applied a cast, he pronounced Holly fit enough to go home. The fracture was not serious, and the cold had done no lasting damage. The heavy blanket of snow had acted as insulation. Extremely sleepy from the emotional ordeal, Holly longed for home and her own soft bed. Her mother and Greg were waiting at the door when she and her father arrived.

Mom had hot chocolate waiting on the stove. As the family sat drinking the fragrant liquid, Holly related the story of her accident. Shyly, she asked their forgiveness for her attitude and her actions of late. She told them of her new committment to Christ and of her desire to live for Him.

"Remember, Mom, how everyone always says we are so much alike? From now on I intend to live a Christian life like you do and . . . in case you hadn't noticed," a mischievous smile lit her weary face. "We are twins in more ways than one." She laid her cast-clad arm on the table next to that of her mother.

Tears flowed unashamedly down more than one face as Jed thanked the Lord for bringing their family safely together again. Four hearts were knit in a renewal of love for each other, but most of all, for their Heavenly Father who had made it all possible.

25

THE NEWCOMER

V. BEN KENDRICK

Jim stood nervously pounding his fist into his glove. It felt a bit strange, being the last one chosen on the physical education class team. The two captains looked over at him. "You can have him, Ken. We'll get by with eight players."

A ripple of laughter came from the players of both teams. Jim's face grew hot with embarrassment. He knew it would be difficult being a Christian in the new high school. He had moved to the area with his family only three weeks earlier, but word had spread around the community about his clean living and Christian testimony.

Just the day before one of the fellows had called out to Jim as he walked into the classroom. "Hey, Preacher Boy! You can stay in this room as long as you leave your religion outside." The room filled with laughter as the new student made his way to his assigned seat.

"Go out and play right field, Preacher," called Ken Stevens, one of the captains. "You'll hit ninth in the lineup."

As Jim made his way to his outfield position he prayed, asking the Lord to help him do his best. "Father, help me to be a testimony for You."

The first batter hit a drive over the third baseman's head for a single. The next man topped a pitch sending a slow roller to short. He barely beat the throw, putting runners on first and second with none out. The next batter was a big kid named Butch. Jim backed up a half dozen steps as the left-handed batter stepped to the plate. The first pitch was fouled off behind first base. The strong batter leveled off on the next pitch, sending it deep into right center field. Jim was off at the crack of the bat. As he neared the fence, he glanced over his left shoulder for the ball. With a desperate last-minute lunge, he left his feet. He caught the ball in the webbing of his glove, and at the same time his body made contact with the fence. Knocked semi-conscious, he fell to the dirt warning track with the ball lodged in his glove. Both runners, thinking the ball had not been caught, ran hard with their heads down.

"Take it," Jim gasped to the center fielder who was leaning over him. "Double them up."

Like a flash, Jim's teammate reached down and took the ball from Jim's glove. His arm unwound like a whip and sent the ball to second base. After touching the bag, the shortstop spun and relayed the ball to the first baseman. The runners stood dumbfounded as they watched themselves being doubled up.

"Triple play!" yelled the first baseman.

"I can't believe it," said Ken Stevens to himself as he ran to the outfield where Jim still lay on the ground. "I didn't know the preacher could play like that."

"Are you all right, Preacher?" asked the center fielder.

"Just a little wind knocked out of me," answered Jim. "I'll be all right. Help me up."

Supported by his teammates, Jim began walking off the effects of the blow. He could hardly believe the change that had taken place in the hearts of the players in such a short time. By the time he reached the bench, he felt like himself again.

"That was the greatest catch I've seen, Preacher," said Ken, shaking Jim's hand. "I didn't know you could play ball."

"Thank you, Ken," responded Jim. "I played for my high school team back in New Jersey."

"When Coach Bentley hears about this, he'll want you to play for our school team. By the way," added the team captain,

140

"I'm changing the batting order. You are moving up to the clean-up spot for us. If you hit like you field, I want you batting fourth."

"I'm still willing to hit ninth," said Jim, who didn't want to push anyone out of his place in the batting order.

"This is only a pick-up game, Preacher. No one's going to mind if I change the order."

The first batter hit a fly out to center field. The next man swung at the first pitch and lined it to the shortstop. Ken Stevens then hit a ground ball past the third baseman. All eyes were on Jim as he stepped to the plate. "Lord," he prayed under his breath, "help me do my best."

The first pitch was a bit outside, and he let it go by. He swung at the next one and sent a hard ground ball past third just inches outside the baseline. The next pitch was a fast ball down the middle. Jim timed his swing perfectly. As soon as he connected, he knew it was a solid hit. The ball took off like a shot, heading deep to left. The left fielder never moved. The ball cleared the fence by fifty feet and landed deep in the trees beyond the ball park. As he ran the bases, Jim was filled with praise. "Thank You, Father," he whispered, "for helping me do my best."

Ken was the first to shake Jim's hand. "You're a winner, Preacher. That was some blast."

As the teams entered the locker room after the game, Coach Bentley was waiting inside the door. "Jim, I want to see you in my office when you get dressed."

The locker room was filled with chatter about Jim's ball playing abilities. One after another came by to congratulate him. Butch Simms was all smiles as he shook Jim's hand.

"That was some catch you made on me, Preacher. You deserved to get it the way you took after it. We need you on our school team."

Coach Bentley looked up from behind his desk when Jim appeared in the doorway. "Hi, Jim. Come on in."

The new student stepped up to the front of the desk. "Thank you, Coach."

"Jim, I was watching you today. We need a left fielder for our ball club. Would you like to try out for the position? From what I saw today, we could use that bat of yours, too."

"I would love to play for the school, Coach. In fact, I was going to ask you today if I could come out to practice."

"You sure can, Jim. Can you come out tonight?"

Jim thought for a moment. "Tonight is prayer meeting at our church. I work with the young people and tonight we are giving our awards. It's the last of the youth programs until fall."

Coach Bentley couldn't believe what he had heard from the strapping young man. "Did you say prayer meeting?"

"Yes, Sir," responded Jim. "You see, Sir, I'm a Christian. I've accepted Jesus as my Savior. I always go to church."

"Come out for a little while after school, Jim. I'll see that you leave on time to get to church. I think it will be good to have a fellow like you on the team. We all need a little religion or whatever it is."

"Thank you, Coach. I'll be there." As Jim was leaving, he turned around to speak once more to the high school coach. "I really don't have religion, Coach Bentley. I have Christ as my Savior. I would love to share some things with you about Him someday when you have time."

"You'll have plenty of time for that, Jim. Maybe you can help all of us to know God better."

Jim had just gone through the door when Coach Bentley called to him. He turned and stepped into the doorway of the office. "I just wanted to say, Jim, that as long as you play ball the way I saw you play it today, I'll listen to you any time you want to talk with me."

"Thank you, Coach. You can count on me to do my best."

Jim went back to his locker to pick up his books. There, to his surprise, he found a number of players from both teams. They had waited to congratulate him for his hitting and fielding during the game. As he left the locker room, he was accompanied by several new friends; he knew there were interesting days ahead for him. His baseball talent had once again opened doors of opportunities for him to witness about his Lord.

142

26

THE FORCEPS

NINA KENDRICK

"Landji, have you seen my other dental forceps?" Allison called as she bent over a barrel, carefully packing it with dispensary supplies.

The tall black man, perspiration dripping from his handsome face, was going over the shiny instruments which lay on a white sheet spread over four barrels which were already filled to the brim. The hot afternoon sun was quickly drying any moisture which might have lingered after each piece of equipment was thoroughly washed and dried.

"No, Miss, I haven't seen it since the last time you used it two or three months ago. That was when you pulled Chief Yabende's tooth there in his village. Do you remember that day?"

"Yes, I remember now, I seem to recall putting it back in my bag, but then . . . I could be mistaken." Her forehead wrinkled as she tried to remember the incident, then her pleasant face broke into a wide smile. "We could have left it there," she mused. "Let's hope none of the children are trying to pull each other's teeth!"

Landji chuckled as his mind's eye pictured several round faces, mouths spread in toothless grins. The thought kept a smile on his lips throughout the afternoon.

By five-thirty the last barrel was completed. There was just time to get them into the store room before the sun dropped behind the hills and darkness fell like a blanket as it does in the tropics.

"Well, Landji, we made it! When we started this morning, I wasn't at all sure that we would finish by this evening. Tomorrow we'll finish up in the house, get the clothes washed and be ready to leave at sunrise Wednesday. The Kendalls will be happy to get the pickup I'm selling to them, right on time."

Vern and Nan Kendall were new missionaries who had spent their first two years on the field without a vehicle. They had been overjoyed when the opportunity arose to buy the nurse's truck. It was furlough time for Allison, and she would be leaving in a few days for a much needed rest in the United States. The last few days are always hectic, and in spite of her bone weariness, she tossed and turned throughout the hot night. She rehearsed over and over the tasks that remained for the next day. Intertwined with these thoughts, the puzzle of the missing forceps nagged at her memory.

Dark circles rimmed the nurse's eyes as she splashed cold water on her face before dawn two mornings later. Her fellow missionaries noticed and were happy that this was her day to leave the station in spite of the sadness of parting.

Several hours later the travelers, weary from the rough roads and intense heat, arrived at the mission station which was located near the airport. The following day was filled with securing necessary papers prior to departure. It was with deep relief that she finally surrendered the pickup keys to the Kendall family and boarded the plane for Paris, her first stop.

The week following, Vern pushed open the screen door of their tiny house on the little, bush mission station. "Nan, look what I found under the seat of the truck. I wonder if Allison missed it?" He put the dental forceps on the table as his wife came from the kitchen where she had been kneading bread.

"Oh my, I certainly hope she didn't have to leave anyone suffering with a bad tooth. Well, at any rate, she won't be needing this for a while." she said briskly. "I'll just put it away until she returns." Nan got a clean towel from the linen closet

144

and carefully wrapped the forceps, placing the neat bundle on the top shelf where it was promptly forgotten.

The dark green pickup carried the young couple to many villages. It was exciting for them to be able to take the Word of God to places where the gospel had never been heard. They knew they must take every advantage during the dry season. Soon the rains would cut off most roads leading from the mission station.

"The Lord has blessed us abundantly, hasn't He, Nan?" Vern said one night as he dropped wearily into bed. They had just returned from a distant town where they had spent several days.

"He surely has," Nan responded. "Not only did He supply a truck for us to visit the villages but He gave us a cozy home, too." She sighed contentedly, thinking of the small, round, mud-block huts they had to stay in while on the road as well as the hard army cot she had slept on for so many nights.

A few days later the rains began in earnest, and the Kendalls knew that their road trips were finished for the next six months. In a matter of days, the roads were covered with water, cutting any communications with the outside world.

It seemed he had been sleeping only a few minutes one night when Vern heard his wife moaning softly. Thinking perhaps she was dreaming, he quietly called her name then rolled over to waken her. He was alarmed to see Nan sitting on the edge of the bed with her head buried in her hands. A lighted flashlight was beside her. From time to time a low groan escaped her. Frightened, Vern sprang from the bed.

"Nan, what is wrong—are you sick?"

"Oh Vern, I have the most awful toothache. I'm sorry I didn't want to waken you, but it hurts so much." The words ended in a sob.

"I'll get some aspirin; that should help. I'll be right back."

Nan followed his course . . . first the bang of the medicine cabinet door, then the kitchen cupboard for a glass and finally the low thud as he shut the kerosene-run refrigerator after filling the tumbler with cold, filtered water.

He was back in just a few moments, and she gratefully swallowed the aspirin. It took a while but finally the pain dulled enough so she was able to sleep a couple of uneasy hours before daybreak.

Intense pain was the only memory Nan had of the next three days. What could they do? There was no way they could get to the city. The heavy rains had taken care of that. Vern knew by the haggard look on his wife's face how much she suffered though she said very little. She tried to carry on her classes as usual but finally had to tell the children not to come back until she sent them word.

In desperation, Vern sought the advice of their co-workers who lived in the other house on the station.

"Len, what can I do? She can't go on much longer like this, and we can't even get to the city to see a dentist!"

"I have pulled teeth for the Africans, Vern, but I did it only because there was nothing else for me to do. I don't have a forceps, and even if I did, I wouldn't know how to grip with them. We don't even have any novocaine and even if we did, I would hesitate to administer it; I have never attempted that!"

An odd look crossed Vern's face.

"Forceps . . . forceps . . . I remember now! I found a set under the seat of Allison's truck. We put them somewhere. Maybe Nan remembers. Would you be willing to try, Len? That is our only hope!" Without waiting for a reply, he sprinted toward his house.

"Yes, I remember," Nan said dully. "They are on the top shelf of the linen closet. Of course I'll let him pull my tooth, anything is better than this!"

Within the hour, the forceps were sterilized and Len was ready to use the unfamiliar instrument on his co-worker. The three missionaries bowed their heads and asked the Lord to help them. Vern held his wife's head firmly, Len went to work and the offending tooth was removed in record time. The relief was so immediate that Nan felt like a new person.

"Just think," she said with awe, "God prepared all those

months ago for our need of a forceps. Won't Allison be surprised when we tell her?"

Len, who was still shaky from the ordeal of being suddenly thrust into the role of dentist, said solemnly, "My verse for the year has taken on a whole new dimension today. 'I can do all things through Christ who strengtheneth me.' I can't quite believe I had the courage to pull a fellow missionary's tooth and without anesthetic, too."

"Missionaries sure find themselves in some peculiar situations," added Vern chuckling. "Len can now qualify as a bona fide dentist, and of course, I must be the world's finest dental assistant."

"We do have many different experiences," said Nan through a towel which covered her mouth, "but I wouldn't exchange any of it, even if I could. Being an ambassador for Christ is the greatest business in the world. And you know what," she giggled through swollen lips, "When He promised, 'But my God shall supply all your need. . . .' I never expected that a dental forceps would be on top of the list for me this year!"

27

THE BIBLE SCHOOL TRUCK

V. BEN KENDRICK

The green pickup truck slowly came to a stop beneath the blossoming mango tree. A young African boy, followed by several of his companions, ran swiftly across the village toward the vehicle.

"Hello, Mr. Missionary! May I have a ride in your truck?"

The skinny, poorly-clad youngster stood looking up at the white man whose face was framed in the cab window. A smile covered the missionary's face.

"I'll tell you what I'll do, . . . uh. . . ."

"Kondo," spoke the lad. "My name is Kondo."

"Thank you, Kondo. My name is Rev. Winters. I want all of you to listen carefully to what I have to say."

As the missionary spoke, Kondo and his friends crowded up close to hear every word.

"At the mission station this week we are having something very special. It's called Vaction Bible School. If any of you come the entire week without missing one day, I promise you a ride in the truck."

The children clapped their hands and shouted. Other children playing nearby joined the group to see what was going on.

"You mean any of us can come?" asked Kondo.

148

"You are all invited," answered the missionary. "The promise is for all of you."

As soon as the truck left the village, Kondo called the children together. "I am inviting all of you to go with me tomorrow to Bible school. We will leave when the sun is that high over the hill." He pointed to a rise where the sun appeared each morning.

The next day the little grass-roofed church building was filled with the chatter of voices. Betty Winters was surprised to find her class had doubled overnight.

"Good morning, children," she called in her pleasant voice. "It's nice to see so many new faces."

Kondo felt nervous even though he knew most of the kids in the class. Hesitantly he raised his hand to get the teacher's attention.

"Yes, what is it?" she asked, looking over at the new boy.

Kondo stood up. He was surprised to find his knees shaking. His high pitched voice showed his nervousness.

"Mr. Winters invited us to come to Bible school. He stopped in our village yesterday. When I asked him for a ride in his truck, he said he would give a ride to anyone who would attend classes the rest of this week without missing. All but six kids came from my village."

"Oh, that's wonderful," exclaimed the teacher. "We are so glad you are here. What is your name?"

"My name is Kondo, Mrs. Winters."

"Welcome to all of you," Mrs. Winters said, smiling. "I'm so happy to see you today."

The new children were all excited about their new adventure. They talked and laughed all the way back to their village.

Meanwhile, back on the mission station, Betty Winters, too, was very happy. "Just think, Bud, Kondo brought thirty-four children with him. He said there were only six others left in the village, and they might come, too, before the week is over."

The young wife's eyes filled with tears as she spoke. "And listen to this! Kondo and eight others accepted the Lord as their Savior after class."

"That's wonderful!" responded Bud. "And to think, before today we couldn't get anyone from that village to come to church. I'm so glad I stopped yesterday. I remember reading that D. L. Moody had what he called his Sunday school pony. The children who came to Sunday school got a ride on the pony."

"I'm sure the Lord will bless this effort, Bud. That boy, Kondo, is a natural leader among the children."

"He seems to be a real worker, too," added Bud. "I hope I'll have a lot of rides to give on Saturday."

"I hope you do, too," said his wife laughing.

The class buzzed like a bee hive as the new children came every day. Not only had Kondo managed to get all but three of the children from his village, but he invited them from other villages as well. By the time Friday arrived, he had personally brought fifty-seven visitors to Vacation Bible School.

On the last day of the Bible school, the children were surprised to see Mr. Winters come with his wife.

"I have asked Mr. Winters to read the names of those who earned a ride in the truck and to give you some instructions."

The children responded by clapping their hands. One by one each child rose to his feet as his name was called.

"That's the last one," Bud said, folding the paper. "There are thirty-three in all."

The students listened carefully as he spoke. "Mrs. Winters tells me that this Bible school has been the largest one we've ever had. We especially want to thank Kondo for all the hard work he has done is making this such a good week."

Bud hesitated a moment and then continued. "I am wondering if any of you would object if I gave everyone a ride tomorrow?"

The smiling faces showed approval. The missionary turned to Kondo. "Since you did the most work this week, Kondo, what do you think of my suggestion?"

"You are very kind, Mr. Winters, to want to do that for all of us." As the lad spoke, the other children clicked their tongues to show their agreement.

"There is something in my heart which I want to say,"

continued the African boy. "I really don't need a ride in the truck tomorrow. You see, Mr. Winters, I've accepted Jesus as my Savior this week. I've also learned a lot about God's Word. You have done so much for us already, Mr. Winters. You don't have to give us a ride in the truck. You have more important things to do."

When Kondo finished speaking, the children shouted their approval for what he had said. A lump formed in Bud's throat. He realized the class was speaking out as one voice.

"Thank you, Kondo. I know your words come from your heart. However, Mrs. Winters and I really want to do something special for all of you. We want to give each one a ride in the truck tomorrow, as well as a feast. The rides begin at nine o'clock. How does that sound?"

The response from the class was deafening. Kondo's heart nearly burst to see his friends so happy.

The next day, everyone was on time to begin the rides, and they shouted and squealed with delight. At noon, they all sat down in the shade of a giant tree. Each one received a paper plate heaped with chicken, corn and manioc. The smacking of lips was their tribal way of showing their delight at the good-tasting food.

Kondo sat beside the missionary couple. "This is a good day, Mr. and Mrs. Winters. And it all started with the promise of a ride in that truck over there."

The young African raised his skinny arm and pointed to the green pickup truck parked in the driveway.

"What is your truck's name. Mr. Winters?"

"It doesn't have a name, Kondo," responded the puzzled missionary.

"We give names to things that are special to us," said Kondo. "If your truck does not have a name, may I give it one?"

"Of course," answered the missionary. "What do you want to call it?"

Kondo looked at the truck for a long time and finally smiled. "I know what we can call it." His face showed his excitement as he spoke. "Let's call it the Bible School Truck!"

151

"From what has happened this week," answered Betty, "it certainly has earned that name."

In the afternoon the children headed back to their villages. Before leaving, Kondo shook hands with his missionary friends and walked over to the pickup. Bud and Betty stood in silence as they watched him. He patted the green truck on the hood.

"Thank you, Bible School Truck. Thank you for your good work this week. If it were not for you, I wouldn't be here."

The young lad then headed back to his village. In his heart he was praying for the day when he would be able to introduce his mother and father to his new Friend—Jesus.

28

A SURPRISE FOR LAURA

NINA KENDRICK

Laura jumped out of bed. She could smell bacon frying, and she was hungry. Mother hadn't called her yet, but she wanted to have plenty of time today. It was her last day of school in America. Her whole family was going to Africa—Mom; Dad; her brother, David and herself. Ever since God had called her parents to be missionaries, Laura had been trying to learn all she could about that far away land that had always seemed so mysterious to her. Excitement, fear and sadness chased round and round in her head. She was excited when she thought of the new things she would see and the new people she would meet, but fearful because she would be experiencing a strange, new country, a new school and a strange race of people. What would it be like? What if she didn't like her new home? The sadness came when she thought about leaving her friends at school and Sunday school. Being so far away from two sets of loving grandparents made her sad, but worst of all Mother said she must leave Topaze, her beautiful Siamese cat.

"How can I live without my kitty," she cried inwardly. "I'll never, never love another cat like I do Topaze!"

Suddenly Laura threw herself on her bed and sobbed into her wadded-up pillow. Mrs. McWayne found her there a few minutes later.

"Laura, honey, what is it?" Gently her mother pulled the weeping child into her arms. "It's Topaze, isn't it?"

"Oh, Mommy, I'll never have such a beautiful cat again. I'll miss her so!" She hiccupped. "Maybe the Morrises won't be good to her!"

"Honey, you know the Morrises will treat Topaze just like you do. Why Melinda is so happy to have her. She loves her too. Remember our talk the other day? The Lord will help you if you ask Him to. Let's do it right now."

She felt much better after the short prayer, and suddenly remembered that she was hungry. Apparently that feeling was shared, for through a crack in the door she heard Daddy call, "Hey, isn't anyone going to eat this morning?" Giggling like two conspirators, Mommy and Laura hurried out to the kitchen where Daddy and David sat at the cheery table with knives and forks poised ready for action.

After breakfast she quickly gathered together Topaze's dish, her catnip mouse and a favorite ball of bright red yarn. Scooping the blue-eyed, cream and brown bundle of fur into her arms, she ran down the block to her friend's house. Melinda, who always seemed to know just when to expect her, was waiting at the door.

Without a word, Laura shoved cat, dish and toys into the waiting arms, turned and hurried back to the sidewalk.

"Laura, wait," called her friend. "I want to show you the nice bed I've made for Topaze." Pretending she hadn't heard, the sad little girl hastened home.

Sadness was swallowed up by excitement during the next few weeks. The McWaynes were to visit most of their supporting churches before they finally left. Each one had a special farewell service, and many had receptions for the missionary family. Sometimes Laura felt like her heart was in a whirl, seeing so many new faces and being in so many different places. Often two or three days would pass when she didn't think of Topaze. She wondered if her cat had already forgotten her. When she mentioned to her mother that this made her feel guilty, her mother placed her arm lovingly around her shoulders and said, "Laura, have you forgotten that we asked the Lord to help you? Don't you suppose this is His way of answering our prayer?"

Finally the day came for a last, quick visit to their hometown. They were to take the plane to their new, far-away home in just two days. Their lovely house was already rented to another family, so this time they would stay with Grandma and Grandpa Evans. Laura was glad they didn't live too far away from Melinda because she just had to see her best friend again. She also wanted to see if Topaze still remembered her.

It seemed that the big cat would burst because she purred so loudly when she saw Laura. Swallowing a lump in her throat, Laura hastily hugged the cat, then she hugged Melinda, and with tears dropping off her chin she hurried away.

"Good-bye, Laura. I'll miss you. I'll write often. I hope you find another cat just like Topaze!" her friend called after her.

But Laura knew there would never be another cat like Topaze. Besides, she just knew that missionaries didn't have Siamese cats! They probably had old ordinary ones just to keep the mice away! Besides she didn't *want* another cat. She only wanted Topaze.

The trip to far away Africa was long and tiring, but there were strange and interesting sights to see all along the way. Excitement hit the highest peak when the plane finally touched down in the land where God had called them to serve Him. Everthing was so different—the sights, the smells, the heat! A large group of missionaries greeted them inside the terminal, and everyone tried to talk at once. Laura, who suddenly realized how tired she was, was glad to climb into the small car that was waiting for them in the parking lot. As Uncle Joe (as the children had quickly learned to call him) expertly steered the car through traffic, he pointed out places of interest along the way.

"You'll be staying with the Kennerly's until you are ready to go up country," he said as they pulled up in front of a large brick house. "It's nearly time for lunch so I'm sure you are eager to get settled."

Laura was close to tears when they entered the cool, attractive home. She was hot, hungry, tired and homesick. It was just too much. She wished they were back in their cozy home in Rosemont.

Sensing the crisis, Aunt Nan, (as she had been introduced to the children) took the small girl by the hand. "Come, Honey, I have something to show you."

Leading the way to a small room where the washing and ironing were done, the new "Aunt" pushed open the swinging door. She pointed to a box in the corner. "Look, Dear, one of them is reserved just for you."

Laura could hardly believe her eyes. In the box were three of the most beautiful Siamese kittens she had ever seen. Falling on her knees beside the box, she picked one up and with wonder breathed, "Why, you are a miniature Topaze. Jesus gave you to me. Oh, I love you. I love you."

Her family, brimming with curiosity, had followed them to the laundry room. Now, looking up into the circle of smiling faces, Laura, who was grinning and hugging the small puff of fur, said, "You know, I think I'm going to like our new home after all!"

29

THE FORGOTTEN PLAQUE

V. BEN KENDRICK

The long, white jet trail stretched across the vast ocean of blue. Jean glanced up as she walked along, but her mind was occupied with the tragedy that struck so unexpectedly that week. It was only about an hour after she and her best friend, Barbara Hale, arrived home from the movies that a phone call informed her that Barbara was dead. She was killed instantly by a truck that blew a tire and ran out of control into her front yard where Barbara was working in the flower bed.

Jean recalled, as she stood at the graveside, how easily it could have been her in that casket. The chills ran through her body as she thought of the past three years and how she had turned her back on God. She knew right then that she had to get back into fellowship with the Lord.

As she approached the church, she wondered what it would be like to be back again among her Christian friends. She entered the familiar door and was greeted by many who knew her. It felt good to be there, but deep in her heart was the nagging thoughts that things were not what they should be between God and her.

The congregation stood for the invitation song. The overwhelming feeling that she was out of the will of the Lord crushed her as if she was in a vise. Jean gripped the back of the pew.

"Oh, God," she cried within her heart, "my life's been a terrible mess." The tears began to flow freely.

"Just as I am! and waiting not. To rid my soul of one dark blot, To Thee, whose blood can cleanse each spot, O, Lamb of God, I come! I come!"

It seemed like Pastor Loggens spoke directly to her as he gave the invitation. "Young man or young lady, if your heart isn't right with the Lord, I beg you to make it right with Him tonight. God knows your heart and He knows your need. Remember, nothing is hid from Him."

Jean quickly moved out into the aisle and made her way to the front of the church. There Pastor Loggens met her.

"My life's not right, she cried. "I want to get straightened out with the Lord."

After the service Jean stayed and spoke with Mrs. Loggens. She told her how she accepted Christ as her Savior as a ten-year-old. It happened when she went to a Sunday school picnic with a friend. Even though her parents protested bitterly, she attended church as faithfully as she could for the next five years, becoming very active in various church activities. She told of the night she gave her life to the Lord for His service. "I knew that God wanted me to be a missionary, and that night I told the Lord to take control of my life and direct it."

"What happened then, Jean?" asked the pastor's wife.

"Well, my parents were so much opposed to religion, I finally gave in to their pressures and tried to forget about God, church, commitment and everything else." Jean wiped her eyes as she talked. "I stopped going to church and put my Bible on a shelf in my closet. I was convicted about what I was doing, but I hardened my heart and tried my best to shut God out of my life."

Jean hesitated and then continued. "The next three years were terrible. I kept drifting farther and farther away from the Lord until I was attending dances and even smoking and drinking. And then things began to happen. After Barb's funeral, I was lost. Looking for something to do, I decided to clean my closet last Friday. While reaching up to get something off the shelf, I knocked my Bible onto the floor, and as I bent over to pick it up, I

158

noticed the book mark sticking out of the place where I last read three years ago. Curiosity got the best of me, and I opened my Bible to that place. My eyes fell on two verses which I had underlined that night in my room."

Jean stopped talking as she fought back the tears. "Let me read the verses to you," she said as she opened her Bible. "They're found in Romans 12:1, 2." She ran her fingers under the words as she read. "I beseech you therefore, brethren, by the mercies of God, that ye present your bodies a living sacrifice, holy, acceptable unto God, which is your reasonable service. And be not conformed to this world: but be ye transformed by the renewing of your mind, that ye may prove what is that good, and acceptable, and perfect, will of God."

The night air felt refreshing as Jean walked home. She felt so clean and good inside. It seemed as if her heart would burst with the joy that filled it. The old feeling of fear gripped her heart as she thought of telling her parents what had happened at church.

"Maybe I shouldn't tell them," she said to herself. "On the other hand," she argued, "I must tell them everything. I'll tell them of my desire to go to Bible college this fall to begin my training to become a missionary." The closer she got to home, the more fearful she became.

"It's about time you're home, Jean," called her mother from the kitchen. "Where have you been and why are you so late?"

"I went to church, Mom," answered Jean, slipping off her jacket.

"You what? You went to church?"

Her father, who had been reading the evening newspaper, stopped and peered over the top of the paper at his daughter. The look on his face was disbelieving.

"I want to go to Bible college this fall, Mom and Dad. I believe the Lord wants me to train to be a missionary."

"A what? What kind of nonsense is that?" exploded her father, standing and dropping the paper into the chair. "Don't tell me you're back to that stuff again! I thought you got away from religion three years ago."

"I'm a Christian, Dad," responded Jean in her quiet voice. "The Lord has saved me, and I want to live my life for Him."

"Jean, I think you'd better go up to your room right now!" commanded her father. "We're your parents and we'll not stand for such disobedience from you."

"But, Dad," cried Jean as she walked toward the stairs, "I'm not disobeying you. I just want to live for the Lord. That's all. I love Him, Dad. I really do."

"That's enough!" said her father in an angry voice. "You talk like a religious fool."

Jean had never seen her father so angry. His face was red as he spoke to her. As she started up the steps, he grabbed her arm—something he had never done before. Fear gripped her heart. "Unless you change your thinking, young lady, you'll have to leave this house—and leave now!"

Jean was in a daze as she packed her suitcase. Her mind was so confused, she hardly knew what she was doing. Her life seemed shattered. She couldn't bear to think that her parents were actually forcing her to leave home because of her love for the Lord.

"Dear Father," she prayed softly, "I don't know where to go or what to do. Please help me, Lord." Jean lifted her head to look around the room. There on the wall above the dresser was a plaque that she hadn't noticed much for the past three years. The words seemed to leap out at her. "I will never leave thee nor forsake thee." An indescribable peace came to her heart. She knew the Lord would take care of her.

A knock on the door startled her. "Jean, it's Dad!"

"Come in, Dad," she called, not knowing what to expect.

Tom Wood opened the door and walked in. The tall, good-looking man walked over to his daughter and took her in his arms. In spite of her eighteen years, Jean felt like the little girl who used to sit on her daddy's lap.

"Jean, Honey, please forget this religion bit and come to your senses. Mom and I'll do anything for you if you will only leave that stuff alone. We don't want you to go, Jean, but you must realize, too, that we don't want religion in this house. I can't

160

believe that my only daughter is trapped in such a snare."

"Dad," spoke Jean looking up into her father's face. "I love you and mom more than words can tell. I want to obey you in every way. But, Dad, Jesus died for me just like He died for you and mom. He saved me and I love Him. Can't you see, Dad? Please try to understand what I'm saying to you."

"I do see what you're saying, Jean." spoke her father. There was bitterness in his voice. "You have chosen your religion over your parents. Yes, I see perfectly what you mean."

He turned as he reached the door. "Good night, Jean. You can stay tonight but you must leave in the morning. I'll give you some money to help you get started on your own." He shook his head as he stepped into the hall. "It's your life, Jean. It's your life."

It was nearly two o'clock when Jean was finally ready for bed. The thought of leaving home left a heaviness in her heart. She looked around her room once again before getting into bed. The words on the little plaque over the dresser caught her eye again. She walked over, took it down and carefully placed it in her suitcase. An hour later as Jean drifted into a deep sleep, the tear stains on her face glistened from the light shining through her window. Unconsciously, she repeated over and over again, "Nor forsake thee . . . Nor forsake thee . . . Nor forsake thee."

30

THIN ICE

V. BEN KENDRICK

"**Come on,** Jim, your parents will never know you went with me."

Jim Cain kicked at a small stone which lay at his feet. The thought of disobeying his parents weighed heavily on his heart. He slowly turned to Ken Strong, the new kid in the neighborhood.

"I can't go, Ken," Jim answered. "My mom and dad would really be hurt if they knew that I had gone ice skating against their wishes. I'm sorry, Ken, but I can't go."

As Jim spoke, he wondered what Ken would think. After all, the new neighbor had been willing to go to church with him.

Ken glanced over at Jim. "I don't understand you, Jim. I went to church with you yesterday. You could at least return the favor. A fine guy you are!"

"Ken, listen to me," said Jim. "I'll go skating with you some other time. Really, Ken, I can't go now."

"All right!" said Ken, half shouting. "Then don't go. And forget about that church bit, too. You can keep all of that religious stuff. I don't want to hear any more of it."

Ken's words cut like a knife into Jim's heart. He remembered how hard he had worked to gain Ken's friendship. The young Christian felt like he was caught in a vice. Surely he couldn't afford to upset his new friend now.

162

"I'll tell you what I'll do, Ken," spoke Jim in a quiet voice. "Meet me at the cove around two o'clock. I can't skate long, but I'll be there."

As Jim walked home, he felt terrible inside. Never before had he done anything like that against his parents. He entered the house and went immediately up to his room. There, he quietly took his skates from the closet and went to a nearby window. Jim noticed his hands were shaking and his forehead was moist. He opened the window quietly and dropped his skates one by one behind a large bush directly underneath him.

"Jim! Dinner's ready." His mother's voice startled him.

All through the meal Jim thought of his disobedience. He wondered what he could say when it came time for him to leave the house.

"I'll be back in about an hour, Mom," called Jim as he reached the back door. "I'm going over to Ken's house to invite him to church Wednesday night."

Jim made his way quickly to the bush and picked up his skates. Looking back to make sure no one was looking, he ran across the street and walked quickly down the sidewalk toward the cove.

"Hi, Jim!" called Ken, who was already on the ice. "I thought you had chickened out on me."

Jim felt a bit rusty as this was the first ice of the season, but with each stride, he gained confidence. "Come on, Ken, I'll race you to the other side."

Ken was surprised to see how well Jim skated. He knew he didn't have a chance to beat his friend as Jim was already a good one hundred feet ahead of him. As Jim approached the middle of the cove, he noticed the ice was becoming much thinner. It began to move under his weight, and he decided he'd better head back. Before he could turn, the teenager crashed through the ice and disappeared under the water. Quickly he pushed himself up, knowing he had to find the hole in the ice. Jim reached up only to find the ice covered him.

"I'm going to drown," he thought to himself. "Lord, help me," he prayed. After what seemed to be an eternity, Jim bobbed up through the hole just as he felt his lungs would burst.

"Help!" he called from his icy prison. "Help!"

"Grab hold, Jim," called Ken as he lay on his stomach and stretched out his coat as far as he could.

Jim seized the coat sleeve and hung on for his life. The ice under Ken was so thin he knew he also could crash through at any moment.

"Hold on fellows, I'm coming." It was Tom Banks, Jim's friend from church.

It was difficult for Tom to walk across the ice with his shoes, but he finally moved close enough to grab Ken's feet. With several strong pulls he managed to get both boys back on solid ice again. They quickly headed for shore.

"I'm freezing," shivered Jim.

"We'll go to Smith's gas station," said Tom, "where you can get warm. There's a phone there and we can call your parents."

The phone rang at the Cain home and Jim's father got up from his living room chair to answer it.

"He what?" said Sam Cain. "Thank you, Tom. We'll be right over." Jim's father looked across the room at Mrs. Cain. "Jim went ice skating and fell through the ice. He's down at Smith's gas station waiting for us."

Within minutes Jim's parents had gathered warm clothing and a couple of blankets and headed for the gas station.

As he dressed, Jim could see the hurt look in his father's eyes. "Dad, I'm sorry for what I've done. I lied to you and mom." Jim's eyes filled with tears as he moved toward his father. "Forgive me, Dad. I've never done anything like this before to you and mom."

The tears began dripping from Jim's chin. "I've sinned against the Lord, Dad. I feel so terrible."

Sam Cain put his arm around his son's shoulders. "I forgive you, Jim. We'll talk about it after we get home." Jim knew his disobedience would leave a scar on his memory for the rest of his life.

Later that night there was a knock at the Cain's front door.

164

The surprise on Edith Cain's face was obvious as she opened the door. There stood Ken Strong.

"Come in, Ken," said Mrs. Cain. "Jim and his father are in the front room. Please go in."

"Mr. Cain," said Ken in a broken voice. "This whole thing was my fault. You see, I asked Jim to go skating and when he refused, I told him to forget about me going to church again. It was only after that that he told me he would go skating with me."

"I was wrong in what I did, Ken" said Jim. "I sinned against the Lord as well as disobeyed my parents. I set a poor example for you, too. A Christian should not act the way I did. I'm sorry, Ken."

The new neighbor stuck his hand out to Jim. "It doesn't seem right that you're the one who got hurt. After all, you were doing it for me." Ken hesitated a bit. "I guess what I really need, Jim, is to know the God you folks know, the God the preacher talked about yesterday morning."

Sam Cain smiled at his wife.

"I really mean it," Ken continued. "You people are different. Your lives are different."

Within minutes the four were on their knees as Ken asked Christ to forgive him of his sins and save him. His prayer was a simple one, but gave real evidence of his desire to be God's child.

As Ken was leaving a short time later, Jim walked with him to the door. Their conversation centered on the Lord's goodness to them that day.

"In spite of my disobedience," said Jim, "God spared my life and brought you to Himself."

"That's right, Jim," added Ken as he walked down the porch steps. "I guess you could say we have both been walking on thin ice."

31

NEVER ON FURLOUGH

V. BEN KENDRICK

Dave Green stood with bowed head during the invitation. The look on his face revealed his serious thinking. "Dear Lord, I want to be a good witness for you here at home. Our neighborhood is filled with many opportunities. Help me to take advantage of them for Your glory."

Dave and Dottie Green had just returned from Africa where they completed their fifth term of service. Since their first day in their new neighborhood, they had sensed the need for some kind of an outreach with the gospel. Actually, for the veteran missionary couple, it was like moving from one mission field to another.

When the church service ended, Dave and Dottie made their way to the front door of the church, greeting friends and strangers alike as they went. Dave was unusually quiet as they walked to their car in the back parking lot. Instead of starting the car immediately, Dave reached across the front seat and took his wife's hand.

"Dottie, my heart is especially burdened tonight for the people in our neighborhood." He paused for a moment as a lump formed in his throat. "I think we should begin a Bible club in our home. We can have just as much a ministry here as we did in Africa. This is our mission field during this furlough year."

Dottie, who was watching her husband's expressions as he talked, shared the burden of his heart. She, too, saw the great need.

"You know I'm with you one hundred percent, Dave," she said in her soft voice. "I'd love to teach a children's Bible class in our neighborhood. In fact," she continued, "I was going to say something to you yesterday about starting one."

The Greens were always open to challenges to reach the lost with the gospel. Dottie's burden showed in her prayer that night as she and Dave knelt beside their bed.

"Dear Father, we believe that You challenged our hearts for our neighborhood. Lead us, Lord, in getting a Bible club started. Help us, too, to reach the parents of the children."

The next morning the excited couple talked about the possibilities that faced them. Dave had just finished drinking the last of his coffee when the doorbell rang.

"I'll get it," he said, pushing away from the table. Through the screen door he saw Bill Mitten, their paper boy. His thoughts immediately returned to the night before, during the invitation. He thought of his prayer, asking God to help him reach the neighborhood with the gospel. He looked at the young man standing on the porch and realized that he was facing a soul which would spend eternity either in Heaven or in hell. As far as Dave knew, Bill Mitten was lost. He walked to the door, knowing he had to say something to the young man about his spiritual need.

"Hello, Bill. How much do I owe you?"

"Same as always, Mr. Green," answered the friendly paper boy.

The thought of Bill not knowing Christ weighed heavily on the missionary's heart. The young man took the money and stuffed it into his pocket.

"Thank you, Mr. Green. Have a nice day."

"Wait, Bill!" called Dave, reaching out to put his hand on the lad's shoulder. "Do you have a few minutes to talk with me about something very important?"

Surprised, Bill looked up at Dave. "Sure, Mr. Green. I'm not in any hurry this morning."

Even though the missionary had witnessed to hundreds of people about the Lord down through the years, he was mindful of his own weakness. In his heart he prayed for just the right words to say to the young boy.

"Bill, what do you know about Jesus?"

Bill's face immediately took on a serious look. "Some people say He's the Lord, Mr. Green, but that's all I know about Him."

Dave immediately knew he was looking into the face of one who was lost.

"He is Lord, Bill. In fact, He is my Lord and my Savior." Dave went on to tell how God's Word says that 'all have sinned and come short of the glory of God' and that 'the wages of sin is death.' Bill stood attentively, drinking in every word. As he spoke, Dave noticed the increasingly serious look on the lad's face.

The paper boy looked up at Dave. "You mean, Mr. Green, that Jesus, God's Son, died on the cross for my sins?"

"That's right, Bill. Jesus died for your sins, and if you will believe that He did this for you and accept Him into your heart as your Savior, He will give you everlasting life."

"Wow!" exclaimed Bill. "That's great. I've never heard anything like this before."

"The Bible says, Bill, 'there is none other name under heaven given among men, whereby we must be saved.' In other words, you can't receive everlasting life any other way except by receiving Jesus as your Savior."

"You know something, Mr. Green? I know I'm a sinner just like the Bible says. I really do need Jesus as my Savior. Mr. Green, how can I accept Him? Can . . . can I do it now or do I have to go to church to do it?"

"You can accept Him right here, Bill. You can ask Him to become your Savior now . . . right here on the porch. Just ask God to forgive you of your sins and to save you."

"Then I want to do it now," said Bill. "God," prayed Bill, nervously, "I ask you to forgive me of my sins and save me. I've done so many bad things and I'm glad that You will forgive me."

168

Dave wiped away the tears as he listened to Bill pray. God had answered his prayers and given him opportunity to lead his first neighbor to Christ. After Bill prayed, Dave prayed, asking the Lord to help the new Christian be a witness for Him. When the missionary finished praying, Bill reached out to shake his hand. "Thank you, Mr. Green. Thank you for taking the time to tell me about Jesus today."

Dave watched as the paper boy walked out of the yard. God performed a miracle right there on the front porch. He waited until Bill was out of sight and then walked quickly into the house. A big smile spread across his face. His heart seemed as though it would burst with joy.

"Dottie!" he called, excitedly. "Guess what happened just now?"

"I don't know," she answered, "but whatever it was, it must be terrific."

Dave then told his wife what had taken place on the front porch. "Just think," he said, "we asked the Lord to help us reach our neighborhood for Him and already He has given us a soul."

"That's wonderful," said the beaming housewife. "It looks like the Lord wants us to begin that Bible club right away. We will start with our first contact, Bill Mitten."

Two doors down the street, Bill was so excited about what had happened to him, he rang the doorbell and waited a moment before he remembered that he had already collected from that house earlier that morning.

32

THE ACCIDENT

NINA KENDRICK

That Sunday, the hot afternoon sun filtered in through the slats of the hospital window. The heat and the dryness made Etienne's throat feel scratchy and his lips were cracked. The monotonous drone of a fly made him drowsy. The beat of African music, which blared from a radio, drifted from the room down the corridor.

Etienne had been in the hospital for over six weeks. He had nothing to read. There wasn't much to read in his tribal language, and his knowledge of French was very limited. Daydreaming helped to pass the time. He remembered that first day when he had awakened in this room. His head ached and felt as if it were detached from the rest of his body, and he had no feeling in his hands or his feet.

His mother sat by his side. She had never shown him much affection, for she was always busy with the younger children and her work in the garden. He knew this was important—after all, they did have to eat—but sometimes he wondered if she loved him. That day when he saw the anxious look in her eyes, he knew that she did. He remembered how he had fallen asleep then, happy in the assurance of her love. It all seemed so long ago.

He wished his mother were here now. She had come often

at first when he was so sick, but as he began to improve her visits were less frequent. She couldn't neglect her garden and the small children any longer. He used to help her with Dimanche and Suzanne and tiny Eli, but now . . . Etienne recalled how he had drifted in and out of sleep—for how long, he couldn't remember.

Abruptly, he snapped out of his reverie. From his fourth floor room, he could hear excited chatter rising from the parking lot far below. Last Sunday he had heard the same thing. The nurse passing by, told him that a crowd had gathered to see some missionaries who had come to visit the patients and give them papers. A fair hope trembled in Etienne's heart. Maybe— just maybe—today they would visit his floor!

Once again sleep overcame the injured boy, and in his subconscious state, he was back in his village. Pascale, his best friend, had just returned from the city. He had a job as a house-boy in the home of a European family. This was the day for which they had waited so long. Yesterday Pascale and the other house help had pooled their wages so that the final payment could be made on the shiny new motorcycle. Next week, Assana would get all of the money. He needed it to pay for a new wristwatch. Etienne wasn't sure about such a system, but it seemed to work. After all, Pascale had his new motorcycle! And he, Etienne, was to have the first ride!

The buzzing fly in his hospital room blended with the sound of the cycle as memory took him skimming over the bumpy road, perched on the seat behind his friend. The hot breeze coming in at the window fanned his face as it had that day. Had anything ever been this exciting before? His heart beat fast each time Pascale accelerated a bit more. This was the life! How he loved it!

Pascale made a broad turn in a nearby village. With a flourish, the two boys waved and grinned at the large circle of spectators. Then, with a loud roar, they were off again heading toward home.

Neither of them saw the pickup until it was too late. Traveling at a high rate of speed, it was careening to their side of the road as it rounded a curve. To avoid a head-on collision, Pascale turned sharply and the two boys were pitched into a deep ravine.

Etienne remembered very little about what followed. He dimly recalled seeing Pascale sprawled on the ground.

He could not remember being picked up by two men and taken to the hospital in the pickup. He had regained consciousness when the doctors were working over his badly broken and bruised body, but the pain was so great that darkness thankfully obliterated the memory. The next thing he remembered was his mother sitting beside his bed.

Now Etienne's thoughts awakened him to the present. He could hear the soft murmur of voices in the room next door. His neighbor must have company. How nice it would be to have a visitor! The oppressive heat made it difficult for Etienne to stay fully awake. Hot tears made his eyelids prickle. His memory, in spite of the fact that he had tried to blot it out, returned to the morning when they had told him what had happened to his friend. Could it be possible that he would never see Pascale again? Was it true that his neck had been broken and that he had died instantly? How could he face the future without Pascale? They had done so many things together. A moan escaped Etienne.

Softly, the door to his room creaked open. His eyes flew open and his heart did a little skipping. Someone had come to see him! It took a while for his eyes to become accustomed to the bright light from the doorway. A soft voice spoke to Etienne in his own language.

"Hello, Son, may I speak to you for a few moments?"

The injured boy was startled to see a lovely white lady with touches of gray in her brown, wavy hair. What could this pretty lady be doing in his hospital room? Why would she come to see him? From the straw bag on her arm she extracted a black Book and some colored pamphlets.

"What is your name?" she asked in a musical voice. "Etienne? That's a good name. Would you like something to read? These booklets tell about Jesus. Have you ever heard about Him?"

172

The boy was surprised to see that the papers were in his own language. "Jesus!" He had heard that name once before when Pascale had tried to tell him what had happened to him. It had something to do with Someone called Jesus. He hadn't been very interested then. In fact, his face burned as he recalled how rude he had been to Pascale.

The soft voice cut into his thoughts. The lady very carefully explained to Etienne how Jesus had come to earth as a tiny Baby. When Jesus was a grown Man, He had died on the cross for the sins of the whole world. And now, if Etienne would believe on the Lord Jesus and accept Him as his own Savior, his sins would be washed away. Etienne would become a new creation with the assurance of a home in Heaven forever.

"Etienne," she gently asked, "wouldn't you like to know Jesus as your Savior? Will you ask Him to come into your heart right now?"

Etienne almost shouted, "Yes, I will! I want Him to be my Savior. What do I have to do?"

The kind woman explained how to ask the Lord Jesus to forgive his sins and to accept Him as his Savior. She helped him pray, having him repeat the words after her. He couldn't explain it, but now he knew he was different. For the first time since he had awakened in the hospital, his heart was free from that dreadful ache. Now, he thought, I know what Pascale was trying to tell me. Now I know why he seemed so different.

Almost like a light exploding inside his head, the thought occurred to him, I thought I would never see my friend Pascale again, and now I know I will because he knew Jesus!

The missionary left a Bible and some more tracts and promised to return the following Sunday.

"That is, if I'm still here," grinned Etienne, displaying white teeth in a happy, shining face. "I have something to live for now. I want all of my family to hear about the Lord. I must get well fast so I can go and tell them. I can even be thankful for the accident. Otherwise, I might never have kept quiet long enough to listen to the story of Jesus.

33

WHY AFRICA, FRITZ?

V. BEN KENDRICK

The roar of the rain on the aluminum roof was deafening in the room below. "I've never seen it rain so hard," shouted Carol. Her words trailed off into the din. A bolt of lightning crashed nearby, causing the lights to flicker.

"This sure is a bad one," responded Bob, looking out the window. "That darkness out there reminds me of what it must be like without Christ. I can't help but think of Fritz."

"I'm sure the Lord brought him into our lives for a purpose," said Carol.

Bob turned to his wife who was sitting a few feet away. "Maybe one of these days we will have the joy of . . ."

"Oh! Oh!" gasped Carol. "There go the lights."

Bob picked up a nearby flashlight and sent a beam of light across the darkened room. "Where are the candles, Carol? I think our light plant has been hit by lightning."

Even though the missionary couple were in their first rainy season in Africa, they already knew the destructive force of the powerful tropical storms.

"I hope there's not too much damage to the generator," spoke Bob, as he sat down beside his frightened wife. "I keep thinking about Fritz. What a wonderful joy it would be to see our German friend come to know Christ as his Savior."

"It sure would be a joy," echoed Carol.

That night before going to bed, the young couple prayed for Fritz. "Father," prayed Bob, "help us to be a witness to Fritz. May he come to know You soon."

The next morning Bob was down at the motor house early. He looked the generator over and then pushed the starter button. Nothing happened.

"It must be in the electrical system," he whispered to himself. Using his tester, he found that a coil had burned out.

"What happened?" questioned Carol as Bob walked into the house fifteen minutes later.

"I think it's a coil. I'll go see Fritz right after breakfast. If there is a coil in town, his store should have it."

Immediately after breakfast, Bob went on his errand. "Are you sure it's the right part, Fritz?" asked the missionary as he fingered the coil in his hands. The young German clerk looked up from the parts manual to which he had referred.

"Sure, it will work, Bob. If your problem is what you say it is, it will work." Fritz hesitated and then continued. "There might be something else burned out, too, but take this for now."

Fritz Zimmer had been introduced to Bob five months earlier by a French friend. Little by little, Bob had gained Fritz's confidence, and they were becoming very good friends.

"By the way, Bob," Fritz added, "if you still have trouble after you put the coil in, let me know. I'll come out and help you."

"Thanks, Fritz. I'll be sure to call you if it doesn't work out."

As Bob walked to his car, he was puzzled about his German friend. Why would such a young, intelligent technician like Fritz choose to work in the heart of Africa when he could have any number of good paying jobs in West Germany? This question had been in Bob's mind since the day he first met Fritz.

Back at the station Bob began the job of replacing the coil. The missionary found a number of complications and spent more time on the light plant than he had planned. Finally, the last wire was fastened and Bob gave a sigh of relief.

"Hello, Bob!" came a familiar voice from outside.

"Why, hello, Fritz. What brings you out from the store?"

"I just wanted to check to see if you got your generator repaired," replied Fritz, stepping inside the shed. "I knew you were a bit concerned when you were at the store this morning."

"Well, thank you for coming, Fritz. That is very thoughtful of you. Let's push the starter button and see what happens."

The engine started immediately, and the bulb hanging from the ceiling shone brightly.

"I guess your worries are over, Bob," said the German, laughing. "Any time you need help, just give me a call."

The two men shook hands and Fritz turned to go to his car.

"Fritz!" called Bob. "I'd like to invite you to come out tonight, but Ambassador and Mrs. White are coming for the evening. I promised to show some slides of our work."

"Thank you, Bob. I'll take you up on that invitation some time."

"Well, since we're talking about it, let's set a date. How about Sunday noon? Maybe you could even go to church with us. It's a national church and they speak in Sango, but I'm sure you would enjoy it."

"That sounds interesting. I'd love to go with you. I've always wondered how the Africans conduct their church service."

"We'll leave at eight o'clock Sunday morning. It will take us about an hour to get there." Bob was trying to keep his excitement from showing in his voice.

The two men shook hands and Bob hurried up the path to the house. He was anxious to share the good news with Carol.

Fritz was much in the prayers of his American friends the next two days. Bob saw him twice before Sunday and came away each time with a greater burden for the friendly German.

Sunday morning was a busy time at the mission station. Fritz arrived right at eight o'clock and the three set off immediately for the outstation church. The service started soon after the foreign guests arrived. Even though Fritz didn't know the songs or the Sango language, he tried to sing along with the African Christians. He sat and listened to every word, surprised that the Africans could carry on their own worship service so expertly. All the way home, Fritz talked about the service. In his heart he knew that those Africans and his American missionary friends possessed something he didn't have. Arriving at the mission station, Fritz and Bob chatted in the front room while Carol put the food on the table.

"Come and get it!" she called as she entered, carrying a bowl of mashed potatoes.

Even as Bob prayed, he sensed that their German friend was doing some serious thinking about his spiritual condition. Several times during the meal Fritz mentioned how good the food tasted. "Thank you, Carol. That was a wonderful meal," said the guest as he moved away from the table.

"You are welcome, Fritz," replied Carol. "You must come more often. We'd love to have you."

A short time later the visitor excused himself and got up to leave. He shook hands with his hosts and headed for the door.

"By the way," said Bob, "you're welcome to stay this afternoon and have the evening meal with us. We missionaries get together for the Sunday evening meal and then have a service where we sing and one of us speaks. Would you like to stay, Fritz?"

"Well, only if I'm not imposing."

"Not at all," answered Bob.

Before long the two men were in the office where Bob showed his friend his coin collection. As she stood beside the kitchen sink where she was washing dishes, Carol prayed that Fritz would be saved. "Dear Lord, please guide Bob as he spends this time with Fritz. Give him the opportunity to witness. Put the right words in his mouth."

As the men finished looking at the collection, the young guest turned to leave the room.

"Fritz," said Bob, putting his hand on his friend's shoulder, "there's something I'd like to ask you before we join Carol."

"What is it, Bob?"

"It's the most important question in the world, Fritz. When you die, where are you going to spend eternity?"

177

The German looked somewhat startled at the missionary. "I . . . I really don't know. I must admit that I've often thought about it. I don't know if anyone can know that."

"Well, Fritz, the Bible says, 'For all have sinned and come short of the glory of God.' " Bob opened up a Bible which was lying on his desk. "It reads here, 'For the wages of sin is death, but the gift of God is eternal life through Jesus Christ, our Lord.' "

"You mean, Bob, that I'm a sinner and my sins will result in death?"

"That's right, Fritz. The Bible speaks of a spiritual death. That's separation from God forever. There had to be a price paid for your sin or there would be no hope. That's why Jesus died on the cross. He paid the full and complete penalty for your sins. He'll save you and forgive you of your sins if you'll accept Him as your Savior."

"How do I do it, Bob?"

Within minutes the two men bowed their heads as Fritz Zimmer asked Christ to save him. After his decision he excitedly hurried to the kitchen to tell Carol what he had done.

"That's wonderful, Fritz. I'm so happy." Carol wiped away a tear which made its way down her face.

That night in the service, the visitor gave his testimony. "I don't know how to say what I want," said the German in a halting voice. "You see, I'm not a preacher. I do know tonight that Christ is my Savior and that I've got a lot to learn about Him and the Bible. I know you are my friends and I ask you all to pray for me."

When Fritz finished, his American friends around the room were smiling through their tears.

"I'm sorry to make you all cry like this," continued the new Christian. "I hope I haven't hurt anyone's feelings."

"Not at all, Fritz," laughed Bob. "We're just filled with happiness that you've accepted Jesus as your Savior."

As Bob and Carol walked with their friend to his car after the service, Fritz spoke freely about himself. "I've often wondered why I came to the heart of Africa to work. With my training, I could have had any number of good jobs back in Germany. Tonight, I realized why I'm here."

"What is it, Fritz?" asked Bob.

"I believe God directed me to Africa to meet you folks. He brought you into my life." The young German stopped and looked into the star-filled sky. "I believe God brought me to Africa to hear about Him and His love for me."

He then looked into the faces of his friends. "Thank you, Bob and Carol, for your kindness to me. I want to especially thank you for telling me about Jesus."

Bob could not help but think of the many more Fritz Zimmers who had yet to hear the Good News. All of them represented opportunities for eternity there in the heart of Africa.

34

A TIMELY VISIT

V. BEN KENDRICK

Bill noticed the bumper sticker on the car in front. "I think he's a Christian, Mary. Surely no one would have 'Jesus Saves' on their car if they didn't believe it."

Mary Gilbert turned to her husband who was studying the man in the other car. "There's a Bible in the back window, Bill. I'm sure he knows the Lord."

"Well, it would be nice to meet him," responded Bill, "but we have to get off at this next exit, and the ramp is right ahead of us."

As Bill turned on his blinker signal to exit, he was surprised to see the car in front of him signal for the same turn-off. "He's getting off, too, Mary. Maybe he's stopping for gas."

The Gilberts' interest increased as the car pulled into a nearby gas station. Both men stepped out of their cars and glanced toward each other.

"Hi, there," called Bill, walking over to the stranger. "I'm Bill Gilbert. I saw the bumper sticker on your car and I want you to know that I'm a Christian too."

The stranger seemed a bit taken back by Bill's friendly approach. "Glad to meet you, Bill. I'm Jim Scott. I'm afraid you have the wrong person. You see, I'm not a Christian."

"I don't understand, Jim," said Bill, with a puzzled look on his face. "My wife, Mary, was sure she saw a Bible in your car. And then, too, there's that 'Jesus Saves' sticker on your car."

"Oh, that! Let me explain," said Jim. "My wife and two daughters are Christians. This car is the one she usually drives. And the Bible belongs to Susie, my eight-year-old daughter."

"Do you live near here, Jim?" asked Bill.

"Just down the street. In fact, I'd better be going as I'm late now. Jean has invited a visiting preacher and his wife to dinner tonight. I guess they're here for some missionary conference at Grace Baptist Church. Jean's a member there."

Bill grinned and stuck out his hand. "Glad to meet you, Jim. I'm the preacher who is coming to your house for dinner. Come over to the car and meet Mary."

That evening at the dinner table, Jim related to Jean how he met the Gilberts. "And that's how it happened, Honey. Kind of strange, isn't it?"

Jean Scott knew the Lord too well to think that things like that just happened.

"Hey, Jim," interjected Bill, "I noticed you have several golf trophies around the house. You must be pretty good at it."

"Well, let's say I play at it," laughed Jim. "I've been in a few tournaments. In fact," he continued, "you may not believe this, but I even got into a church tournament some time ago. I've never played with a nicer group of men."

"That's great," said Bill. "It just may be that I know some of the fellows. I've quite a few friends who play golf and before I developed a leg problem, I used to knock the ball around, too."

"That's the truth," laughed Mary, "from what I've heard, that's about all you did."

"OK," grinned Bill, "at least I got to the place where I could hit the ball on the first swing. That's better than some people I know." Bill and Mary looked at each other and laughed.

"All right, Bill, you win. Don't tell anymore on me and my poor golf game."

"Jim," asked Bill, "how would you like to meet some of my golfing friends?"

"I'd love to meet them, Bill. Would they mind playing with a sinner?" said Jim jokingly.

"No, these fellows won't mind that," answered Bill. "You see, Jim, we're all sinners. The Bible says that we're born in sin."

Jim could not get over the friendliness of the visiting missionaries. Deep down in his heart he knew that Christians possessed something that he didn't have. After the meal, Bill and Mary chatted for a few minutes and then excused themselves as they had to unpack their bags before the evening service. The place where they were staying was only a few blocks away. Before leaving, Bill invited Jim to the services.

"They sure are a nice couple," Jim commented as he closed the door.

Jean could sense the excitement in her husband's voice as he told her that Bill was going to contact him about the golf tournament. She was glad that Bill invited Jim to the meetings. Many times through the years, she had asked him to go with her to church, but always received a firm but polite, negative answer. There was a moment of silence.

"Jim," she asked hesitantly, "would you go to church with us tonight? We'd love to have you go with us, Honey. I'm sure you would enjoy hearing Bill tell about his experiences in the Philippines."

Jim was silent as he stood running his hand over the new golf club he had bought that afternoon. Jean patiently waited for his answer.

"All right, I'll go with you. But remember, I go on the condition that we sit in the back and we leave just as soon as it's over."

"That's fine with me, Jim," responded Jean. It was hard for her to contain the joy which flooded her heart.

As Jean cleaned up the table and got the children ready, she kept praising the Lord for this wonderful answer to prayer. She had accepted Christ as her Savior a year after their marriage. Jim was very hostile at first and then softened as the years passed. She had decided early in her Christian life that she would never put pressure on him concerning spiritual matters. She thought it best to pray faithfully for him and be the wife that she knew the Lord wanted her to be.

That night, Jim was rather quiet as he drove the car to the church. As they walked up the front steps together, Jean felt good inside. This was the first time they had gone to church as a family.

"Hi, Jim," greeted Bill with a firm handshake. "Glad you were able to make it."

"Hello, Jim," added Pastor Russell. "It's good to see you."

As she promised, Jean and Jim sat near the back. The service began promptly on time. Jim was impressed with the good singing of the congregation. "They sing like they believe it," he thought to himself.

A duet was sung by two college girls and again, Jim was impressed. He could not help but notice the clean-cut quality of the young ladies. He could see now why Jean sought the fellowship of such people.

Jim listened carefully as Bill spoke. "His message is so practical and makes sense," he whispered to himself. "They're the same things that I've heard from Jean since she became a Christian."

During the invitation Jim felt a tug in his heart to respond to the spiritual need within him. It wasn't a long invitation and soon the service ended. Jean felt sick at heart that Jim had not responded to the invitation in some way. He thanked Bill for the message, made a few comments about their golf conversation and left the church. As they walked to the car, Jean sensed that Jim was thinking about something. He spoke about the message on the way home and how much he had enjoyed it.

"I'll put the children to bed, Jim, and then if you would like, we can have a snack before we go to bed."

"I'll help you, Honey," said Jim. "If it's all right with you, I'd like to talk with you about something."

Fifteen minutes later the young couple sat alone in the den. Again, Jim spoke about the message he had heard that evening.

"Know something, Jean?" He forced a smile as he spoke. Jean had never seen him look so concerned about anything before. "Your words and your life these past years finally broke through to me tonight during the service. I guess it took the visit of Bill and Mary to our home to do it, but I want you to know that I've come to the place where I want to do something about the need in my life."

Jean's eyes filled with tears of joy as she reached over to hold Jim's hand. "Oh, Jim, I'm so happy to hear you say this."

"I'm ready to accept Christ, Jean. Will you pray with me?"

Jim and Jean slipped to their knees as Jim confessed his sins and asked Christ to save him. As she rose to her feet, Jean knew that she had a different husband. She put her arms around him and wept for joy.

"Hey!" said Jim, filled with excitement. "I had better call Bill and Mary and also the pastor. I want them to be the first to know what happened."

"That's wonderful, Jim. This is great news," Bill responded, wiping a tear from his eye.

"And, Bill," added Jim, laughing. "You can tell the tournament leader that Jim Scott, the old golf pro, but new Christian, is anxious to meet his brothers."

"I sure will, Jim," answered Bill with a chuckle. "I'll be sure to do that."

Never before had a snack tasted so good to Jean Scott as it did that evening.

35

NO VACANCY

V. Ben Kendrick

Ted Steele glanced at his watch. "I think we'd better begin looking for a motel room, Pat. I know it's only 4:30 but the traffic is heavy and there could be quite a demand for rooms tonight."

Pat looked up from the motel guidebook through which she was leafing. "Whatever you think best, Ted."

"Maybe I'd better get off at the next exit. If there's nothing there, I'll ask them to call ahead to their next motel and reserve a room."

"I'm sorry, Sir, there just aren't any rooms available. In fact, I've checked with all the motels at this exit and there's not even one room."

"Can you call ahead for us, Miss?" asked a man standing beside Ted.

"Sir, I'd be glad to do that, but I've been calling for customers in both directions since mid-afternoon. There's not one room within fifty miles."

"What'll we do, Pat?" asked Ted as he got back into the car after stopping for the eighth time.

"All I can tell you, Honey, is that the Lord has a room for us somewhere tonight. I don't know where the room is or how we will find it but I know He will direct us to the one He has for us."

"It will take a miracle," said Ted, slowly shaking his head.

"At the last exit a man told me he has been stopping at every motel for the last three hours. And he came from the direction we are headed."

"I know God has a room for us, Ted," Pat assured him. "He'll show us right where it is at just the right time."

In a matter of minutes they were out on the highway again. The couple had been traveling for twelve hours, and signs of fatigue were beginning to show on Ted when a large, green sign came into view.

"We're approaching the bypass, Pat. What do you think we should do? Shall we go into the city and look for a room?"

Pat looked across at her husband whose face showed the strain of the long day. "Let's take the bypass, Ted. There's an exit another ten miles down the road."

"But, Pat, probably hundreds of people have been turned away tonight at that exit."

"You're probably right, Ted, but let's stop anyway. I know the Lord has a room for us, and I don't think He wants us to travel much longer."

"There's the exit sign now," spoke Ted ten miles later. "And there's a motel right nearby. I'll try that one first."

As they drove up in front of the motel office, Ted and Pat noticed the line of people talking to the desk clerk. Ted entered the office and the clerk turned her attention toward him. Ted began hesitantly. "My wife and I have been traveling since early morning, and I'm wondering if you have a room for us."

"I'm sorry, Sir, but we don't have a thing. In fact, we have been filled since early this afternoon."

Ted felt sorry for the young lady. He realized she was helpless to meet the needs of the tired travelers standing before her.

"What about the motels in nearby towns?" Ted asked.

"I'm sorry , Sir, there is nothing in this entire area. We've not seen a night like this in a long time."

The weary traveler surprised himself with his next question. "Would you have any blankets that I could buy? Maybe my wife and I could make a bed in the car."

186

The clerk looked at Ted and smiled as an idea flashed in her mind. "Well," she said slowly, "if you wouldn't mind, we could fix up our conference room for you and your wife. It's not much, but we could put two rollaways in it for you. It has a private wash room, too."

"We'll take it, Miss," replied Ted. "It's a place to sleep, and we really don't need anything fancy."

"You are welcome to it," continued the young lady. "I won't charge you anything for it either. It's with the compliments of the motel. We'll furnish you with linens and towels."

"That's great," said Ted, motioning for Pat to join him. The line of travelers seemed stunned as they heard the conversation.

"Bring your baggage into the office for now," said the clerk. "I'm sure you are hungry, so why don't you go over to our restaurant and have a bite to eat. That will give us time to fix up the conference room for you."

Ted and Pat couldn't help but notice the expressions on the faces of the people standing around them. As they made their way to the restaurant, Ted looked back at the crowd in the office. "There are people in there who would pay almost any amount for a room tonight."

"I think so, too," responded Pat, "but their money is worthless in such a situation as this. There just aren't any rooms."

"This is a miracle," voiced Ted as they entered the restaurant.

"It really is a miracle, Honey," said Pat. "The Lord led us to the right place at just the right time."

No sooner had the excited couple been seated when a waitress came over to their table. "Excuse me, Sir, but are you Mr. Steele?"

"Yes, I'm Ted Steele," answered the surprised traveler.

"There's a telephone call for you. Please follow me."

As Ted walked to the phone he wondered who could be calling him. As far as he knew, no one knew where he and Pat were at that moment.

"Hello!"

"Is this Mr. Steele?" came a lady's voice through the receiver.

"Yes, this is Ted Steele."

"Mr. Steele, this is Carol at the desk. I have good news for you. I just received a cancellation and now you folks can have a regular room."

"That's wonderful, Carol. Shall we come over now?"

"No, that's not necessary. Take your time and enjoy your meal. When you come over, we'll direct you and Mrs. Steele to your room. This will be much better for you than the conference room."

"Isn't this exciting?" said Pat as her husband told her about his conversation with the desk clerk. "It is such a joy to see the Lord work this all out for us."

A short time later, Ted and Pat were back at the desk talking with Carol. "I'm going to have to charge you for this room, Mr. Steele. I hope that is all right with you."

"Of course, Carol. You don't know what this means to us."

Ted stuck his hand into his shirt pocket and pulled out a tract. He reached across the counter and placed it in Carol's hand. "We want you to have this, Carol. There's good news in it for you."

The young lady seemed somewhat surprised at the friendliness of the middle-aged couple. "Thank you, I'll read it when I get a chance."

Ted wanted to continue his conversation with Carol, but a man standing nearby demanded her attention, and a new group of travelers had pulled up to the front door. As they walked to their room, Ted prayed, "Lord, she has Your Word. Please speak to her heart through the tract."

The young lady was very much upon their hearts that night. "Wouldn't it be wonderful," exclaimed Pat, "if Carol would make room in her heart for Jesus like she made room for us tonight?"

Pat's thoughts went back to that night when Joseph and Mary could find no room in the inn. Her heart ached as she thought of the millions like Carol without Christ.

The next morning there was another desk clerk on duty

when Ted and Pat came down for breakfast. "I wonder if Carol read the tract," commented Pat, glancing about hoping to see her somewhere.

"I'm sure she did," responded Ted. "We must leave that with the Lord."

As they ate breakfast, their conversation continued regarding Carol. "I feel bad that we won't see her before we leave," spoke Pat. Ted sensed a note of sadness in his wife's voice.

"Good morning, Mr. and Mrs. Steele!" The couple looked up to see Carol beaming down at them.

Ted stood up to offer her a chair beside them. "Hello, Carol. We were just speaking about you."

"I've been thinking about you folks, too," responded the young lady. "I'm not supposed to come to work today until one o'clock, but I just had to come to see if you were still here. I'm glad I found you."

"We're glad you did, too," said Ted. "What can we do for you?"

"You already did it, Mr. Steele. You see, I read that paper you gave me after I got home last night. In fact, I read it several times. I wanted to call you folks but it was late and I didn't want to bother you."

Ted noticed a tear trickling down his wife's face. "It wouldn't have been any bother, Carol. But, please, go on with your story."

The desk clerk reached into her purse and pulled out the tract. "I want you to see what I wrote on the back of the paper you gave me." She handed it to Ted.

"Praise the Lord," he whispered. "Pat, listen to this." Ted read what was written on the back of the tract. " 'I, Carol Wood, acknowledge that I'm a sinner. I believe that Jesus died for me, and I accept Him as my Savior.' "

"That's why I wanted to call you," said Carol. "I have a girlfriend who is a Christian, and she's been talking to me, too."

"What made you make your decision?" asked Ted.

"I just couldn't get over the fact that you people, who had never seen me before, were interested in me and gave me that paper. I wished I could have talked to you then, but I had too many customers."

"That's what the Lord expects us to do, Carol," spoke up Pat. "We want to share the Good News about Christ with as many people as possible."

"I know you must be in a hurry," said Carol, "but if you have some time to spare, I'd like you to meet my friend, Nan Hart. She talks just like you do. Besides, I want her to meet the people who helped her to help me."

As they left the restaurant, Ted and Pat shared with Carol how God had directed them to find her. "Pat kept assuring me that God would help us find the room He had for us."

"I'm so glad God brought you here last night," said Carol. "He had a vacant room and a vacant heart to fill."

36

TWICE SAVED

NINA KENDRICK

Bright sunlight streamed through the open kitchen window that spring morning. The curtains stirred in the soft, fragrant breeze and bright lights bounced off the whiteness of the stove and refrigerator as the stained glass bluebird hanging on the curtain rod twisted in the gentle wind.

Sam suppressed some of his excitement with difficulty. He knew how his wife, Mary, felt about this day. Timmy, a second grader, was already at the table making short work of a steaming bowl of cereal. Robin, in her high chair, clapped her hands and squealed in delight when she saw her daddy in his sparkling new uniform. Tim was first to speak.

"Wow, Dad, you really look neat. Wait'll I tell the kids at school!"

Mary turned and raised her unsmiling face for his good-morning kiss. Sensing her deep unhappiness, Sam gently placed a finger under her chin and raised her head until he could look into her eyes. "It will be all right, Honey, I promise!" Then he reached over and pulled Robin's ear; he smiled at her shriek of mock pain.

"I saw a robin yesterday but it didn't have cereal all over *its* face!" The shriek turned to giggles as Sam took his place at the cheery table. He was proud of his wife. She always kept the house spotless, cared for the children lovingly and prepared attractive, nourishing meals. If only she shared his enthusiasm for his new job. She knew before they were married that this was his dream. He had wanted to be a policeman ever since he was a little boy. He remembered so well the day Officer Jensen had been at their school to talk to the children about safety. The tall, good-looking man in the blue uniform had become his idol, and he determined then that someday he would follow in those footsteps.

The rigorous training was over; he was now ready for his first day of duty on the force. Mary had never been in favor of this new career. She was more unhappy now that the day had actually arrived. She couldn't understand why he couldn't remain in the factory where he had started out. That was a good job with ample pay.

"I'll worry every minute you are away," she complained. "Why do you have to do such a dangerous job? So many terrible things are happening these days."

When Sam arrived home that evening he kept the whole family, even Mary, in gales of laughter telling them amusing stories of his routine day. It didn't matter that some of the stories were highly embellished; at least his wife had lost some of her tenseness.

After Timmy and Robin were in bed, Sam and Mary sat close together on the living room sofa. "And wouldn't you know it, Honey," he groaned, "I drew some sort of a religious nut for my partner. He even carries a Bible in the glove compartment. I must admit though, he is a great guy even if he is a bit of a fanatic."

"You had better watch out," admonished his wife. "That's the last thing we need in this family—some kind of hocus pocus!"

Together, arms entwined, they climbed the stars. Sam was relieved that Mary seemed to have gotten over some of her bitterness.

The days stretched into months. By mid-summer Sam realized that his partner, Neal Borden, had something that he would very much like to possess. There was an inner peace that Sam envied and longed to have in his own life. The two men had plenty of time to discuss spiritual things as they spent long hours each day in the patrol car.

It was on a hot day in early August when Sam finally realized that Jesus had died for *his* sins. That same day he joyfully received Him into his life and heart. The joy Neal felt at having led his good friend to the Lord reflected brilliantly in his face.

"I feel somewhat like Hannah must have felt about her Samuel. I asked the Lord for you, and He answered my prayers. Sammy boy, you have a fine Bible name—now you will serve Samuel's God just as he did."

The reaction at home was far different. Mary refused to even listen whenever Sam mentioned spiritual things. She became extremely angry when he read Bible stories to Timmy and Robin. The children drank in every word, and it wasn't long until his son invited Jesus into his heart. The two of them grew by leaps and bounds. Together they prayed that Mommy would be saved and that as soon as baby Robin was old enough, she, too, would ask Jesus into her heart.

On his birthday, Sam received a beautiful little leather-bound Bible from Neal. The young policeman was delighted with the gift and slipped it into his shirt pocket.

"I'll carry it here every day. Then I'll always have it when I need it," he grinned. "You've given me something I'll always cherish, Neal. Thanks!"

The little Book was an unfailing solace to Sam. At home the children were his only joy. Mary assumed her former petulant attitude, but with renewed force. She scorned his new-found faith, and at every opportunity she complained about his work. The unhappy woman refused every overture of friendship made by the wives of Sam's co-workers.

"Don't worry, Daddy, Jesus will answer our prayers," consoled Timmy. "Mommy just doesn't understand yet."

Neal's advice was much the same as that of the little boy. "We'll just keep on praying, Sam. God will somehow make her see that He loves *her*, too. My wife and kids are praying. They are anxious to meet your family." They were comforting words, but Sam's heart was still deeply distressed.

The weather remained warm late into September. Sam and Neal were making their usual rounds, late on a Thursday night. They left the patrol car to check a row of stores in a small shopping area, and Neal tried the doors at the front while Sam went to the back to see that all was in order. As he rounded the end of the first store, he was startled to see a flash of light about halfway up the alley. Before he knew what had happened, a shot splintered the silence, and he was knocked to the ground. He heard feet pounding past as Neal ran by him and tackled the surprised thief. After hand-cuffing the frightened young man, he returned to where Sam still lay. His face was white with apprehension as he knelt by his friend.

"Where did he hit you, Sammy? Are you all right?"

Sitting up rather gingerly, his smile a bit wobbly, Sam reached into his shirt pocket. He extracted the little Bible; its lovely cover was marred by the bullet hole which had penetrated nearly to the last page.

"This Book saved my life, Neal. It really *was* there when I needed it. This is the second time I've been saved by His Word. He sure used it in an unexpected way tonight. What a story to tell my grandchildren!"

Mary was by his side later as the doctor examined the ugly bruise on his chest. It was all that remained to tell of his narrow escape. He was pronounced fit enough to go home, and Sam walked hand in hand with his wife down the hospital corridor.

"When Neal called, my world seemed to fall apart. Even though he assured me that you were all right, I was so afraid. All the way to the hospital I thought about what would happen if you were to die." Her voice sank to a tremulous whisper. "I'd never see you again!"

"It's all right, Honey. I'm very much alive. Just look—ouch!" Sam flinched as he flexed his left arm. "Let's not talk any more about it. You drive. Let's get home, in a hurry—I'm starved!"

Mary's voice was urgent now. "No, Sam, we've got to talk about it. You see, if you . . . if you *had* been killed tonight and I

194

knew I'd never see you again . . . oh, Sam, I've been thinking a lot lately. Maybe that's why I've been so hard to get along with. You and Timmy, you seem so—well, different since you found out about this Jesus. I'm not sure, Sam, but I think I'd like to have what you have."

Sam was very quiet the rest of the way home. Mary didn't know it but he was praying that the Lord would use the little Book in his pocket to save one more soul tonight.

37

UNPLANNED INVESTMENT

V. Ben Kendrick

The phone's loud, sharp ring shattered the silence of the office. Steve Wood automatically picked it up. "Hello! Yes, this is Steve. I'll be glad to drop it off on my way home, Mrs. Tanner. Yes, in about twenty minutes. Goodbye, see you later."

Steve placed the phone back in its cradle and rubbed his tired eyes. This sure had been a long day, he thought. Well, I'd better get that refrigerator on the truck.

Steve had planned to have one of his men deliver the appliance the next day, but Mrs. Tanner had to go out of town on business. She was glad that she was able to reach Steve at the store before he left for home. The young businessman had known Mrs. Tanner since his boyhood days. He used to deliver newspapers to her house and usually came away with a pocketful of cookies.

Working quickly with the lift, Steve placed the crate on the truck. Jumping into the cab, he threw the small bag down on the seat beside him. The small bag contained $1,400 which represented the day's receipts.

Within ten minutes, the pickup pulled into Mrs. Tanner's driveway. The elderly lady opened her front door.

"Steve, I'm sorry to cause you this extra work today. You must be very tired after such a long day at the store."

"Don't think anything of it, Mrs. Tanner. I'm glad to do this for you. It won't take long to unload it."

Not wanting to leave the bag of money in the cab, Steve stuck it in his back pocket. He climbed into the back of the truck and unstrapped the huge box from the side rack. As he bent over, the bag of money fell out of his pocket. As he was not able to put it back in his pocket just then, he tossed it onto the roof of the cab.

Within fifteen minutes, Steve had the refrigerator sitting in the place that Mrs. Tanner pointed out to him. It seemed like old times as he reached his hand into the familiar cookie jar before leaving the house.

"It sure will feel good to get into that hot shower," Steve told himself as he turned down his street. "I can hardly wait to tell Jean what a wonderful day we. . . ."

Steve turned to look where the money bag had been on the seat beside him. "Oh, no!" He pulled over to the curb and quickly got out of the cab. His heart sank as he scanned the top of the cab. "It's gone! I've lost $1,400." Steve felt a cold chill run through his body, and goose pimples showed on his arms.

"Lord," he prayed, "please help me find the money."

He turned the truck around and retraced his path. His eyes searched every inch of ground along the side of the road. Mrs. Tanner cried as Steve told her what had happened.

"I'm so sorry, Steve. It's my fault that you lost it."

"It's not your fault, Mrs. Tanner. I just forgot that I tossed it on top of the cab."

Steve continued to scour the route between Mrs. Tanner's house and his house until darkness finally forced him to give up the search.

"The Lord knows all about it, Steve," said Jean as they sat talking after supper. "He can help you find it."

Early the next morning, Steve continued his search, going back and forth over the very familiar route. That day at the office, he called his employees together and told them about his loss and the path that he had taken the night before. The days following, he took every spare moment to go and look for the little green bag.

Five days later, Steve returned home early; he had something on his heart that he wanted to share with Jean. "I really believe, Honey, that if we find that money, we should give it to missions. Only a miracle of the Lord will recover it."

Steve stood looking at the floor. "Our missionary conference starts in two days. Maybe the Lord has saved the money for this conference," said Steve, becoming more excited as he spoke. "There's still some daylight remaining, Jean. I'm going to look for the money while you get supper."

Before he left, the young couple bowed their heads and once again asked the Lord to help them find the money.

The last rays of the sun were just beginning to lose their brightness as Steve moved slowly down the road. He prayed as he drove.

What's that? It wasn't much, just a flash from the sun shining on something in the grass. Steve stopped the truck and backed up to the place where he saw it. He walked slowly, his eyes covered every inch of the ground before him.

Once again there was that same flash. The sun's light reflected from a small brass eyelet. Steve bent over to pick up his precious find. "Thank You, Father," he prayed, "thank You, dear Lord. It's all Yours for missions."

Steve's heart was filled with joy as he told his employees about the money the next day. "The Lord did it!" said Steve to his staff.

The Wood family sat in their usual place on Sunday morning. The speaker was Bud Kendel, veteran missionary from the Central African Republic. Bud and Nan had only three more months left of their furlough.

Pastor Dan Gates walked to the microphone. "The man I'm about to introduce to bring the first message of our conference has been a very dear friend of mine for many years. Bud, I don't mean to embarrass you but I would like to ask you a question: if you could have one special need supplied today, what would you want it to be?"

Bud was taken by surprise. He had never used the pulpit to speak about their financial needs, but since he was asked by the pastor, he saw no reason why he should not tell of the burden that had been upon his heart.

"Well, Pastor, I would have to say that it would be the remaining amount needed to purchase a truck for the field."

"How much do you and Nan need, Bud?"

"We need $1,400, Pastor Gates."

Steve felt Jean's elbow poke him in the ribs. A smile spread across his face. "That's it," he whispered. "That money is for Bud and Nan Kendel." Jean reached over and squeezed his hand.

Immediately after the service, Steve called Pastor Gates aside and told him about the money. The pastor, in turn, called Bud and Nan over and introduced them to Steve and Jean. Within minutes, Steve told the story, beginning with Mrs. Tanner's telephone call and ending with the morning service. The veteran missionary couple were thrilled once again to see God's hand working in their behalf.

"It sure feels wonderful," said Steve, "to be used of the Lord, even if it did cost us $1,400."

"You're mistaken, Steve," spoke up Pastor Gates. "It didn't cost you anything. In fact, you have gained."

"You're so right, Pastor," said Steve. "It is our gain because it's an investment for eternity."

38

ALL IN A DAY'S WORK

V. BEN KENDRICK

Walt Henry looked out the side window of the pickup. "It's really dark out there," he said, glancing across at his two African friends sitting in the cab with him. "They say when it's dark like this the leopards like to come out. Is that true, Kobe?"

The middle-aged African lifted his hands from his lap and cracked his fingers before answering. "They like the dark nights all right, Mr. Henry, but if they're hungry, they'll come out at any time." Kobe hesitated a second and continued. "In fact, they will even come out in the day time."

"Are there any in this area?" questioned Walt.

"Oh, yes," responded Ngoro, who was quietly listening to the conversation. "This region is noted for all kinds of wild game."

Walt did not make it a practice to travel at night in Africa, but because of several unscheduled stops for meetings that afternoon, he found himself five hours behind schedule. Betty Henry and a visiting missionary couple, who left the mission station that morning, planned to meet Walt and his team of African men at sundown in a village which was still ninety miles away. From there they would travel the remainder of the trip together.

"I'm glad I'm not traveling alone along these roads," whispered Walt to himself. The thought of it sent a chill through his body.

"There are lots of lions in this area too, Mr. Henry," said Kobe, stretching out his legs. "I can tell you that those six men in the back of the truck would love to be up here in the cab with us. We've heard a lot of stories about people being caught by animals in these parts."

Suddenly, Walt heard a sound like a shotgun blast. Following the loud noise, the back of the truck on the driver's side dropped almost to the ground. The missionary immediately stopped the pickup. "Oh, no!" said Walt, stepping down from the cab. "I think we're in trouble."

The veteran missionary took his flashlight and soon found the problem. The back mainspring leaf snapped off, allowing the truck bed to fall onto the axle and wheel.

"Now what'll we do?" Walt whispered more to himself than to his traveling companions. "I haven't a replacement leaf, and we are 200 miles from the mission station."

The men in the back jumped out as soon as the truck came to a stop. Some stood guard, looking off into the darkness, while the others surveyed the problem.

"We can fix it, Sir," said Ngoro, showing his filed teeth with a broad smile. "It won't be like you would do back at the station, but we can fix it enough to travel."

"Well," responded Walt, not knowing what to do, "if you can fix it, you have my permission."

The men sprang immediately into action. Four of them armed themselves with machete and knives and disappeared into the darkness. Walt wondered how they could see anything out in the open, let alone in the forest. Once again, he was reminded that these men were experts in their own culture. They often traveled at night without light. Within fifteen minutes they were back at the truck with several bundles of bark strands and a pole about six feet long and seven inches thick. Walt watched in amazement as Ngoro instructed the men to line up along the truck.

"All right," called the respected African, "everybody lift."

The men sang as they counted. On the count of two, they lifted the truck bed and held it while Ngoro and Kobe pushed the pole in under the bed, resting it on the axle. The left back wheel was then pushed forward to make it parallel with the opposite one. Several of the men began tying the pole to the axle and the bed to the pole.

"I wouldn't believe it if I didn't see it," mused Walt.

The team worked like a well-oiled machine and in thirty minutes they were ready to travel. Back in the truck, Walt looked over at his two friends. "You men worked fast to get that job done."

"We didn't say anything to you, Sir, but there was a lion not more than fifty feet from us. The men saw him when they went into the forest to cut the pole."

"A lion!" exclaimed the missionary showing excitement in his voice.

"That's right, Mr. Henry. It must have stepped off the road when it heard us coming and just waited right there in the grass until we left. We're really not afraid of lions as much as we are leopards. They're the most dangerous."

Just as Ngoro finished speaking, the headlights picked up a pair of eyes in the darkness ahead. Within seconds, a huge spotted cat stood before them, fully illuminated by the bright lights.

"What will I do?" asked Walt, stepping on the brake. "I don't want to run into it."

"It's wounded, Mr. Henry and it's out looking for trouble. If it sees the men in the back, it will jump in there after them."

The leopard, although blinded by the headlights, stood its ground in the middle of the road. To try and run over it was too dangerous. Walt knew he couldn't outrun the fierce, wounded beast over the rough road. "He's not going to budge. I'm going to have to shoot it," said the missionary, as he brought the truck to a halt forty feet from the leopard. He took his rifle from the rack and slowly stepped out onto the road. Sensing a battle, the big cat moved quickly into the grass on the side of the road. Walt took a few steps in front of the truck. He didn't want to venture

202

too far, but at the same time felt that he should kill the wounded animal. He waited a few minutes but nothing happened.

"Mister Henry!" called one of the men in a low voice. "Here it is. Turn around."

The frightened missionary turned toward the truck but couldn't see a thing because of the blinding headlights.

"Where is it?" called Walt.

"It's right here," came the soft, excited answer. "It's beside the truck."

When Walt got back to his side of the truck, he looked up into the frightened faces of his African companions.

"Where is it?" he asked again.

Without saying another word, the man pointed to the opposite side of the truck. There, sitting beside the front wheel was the wounded leopard, staring at Walt. The missionary slowly lifted his rifle and without even sighting, pointed it into the face of the big cat. It seemed to Walt that he could touch the leopard with the gun.

"It's going to jump, Mr. Henry," called Ngoro from inside the cab. "Shoot! Shoot!"

As the leopard crouched to spring, Walt squeezed the trigger. The blast was deafening. The giant beast feebly leaped onto the hood and slid off to the ground. It snarled and dashed off into the grass.

Walt's legs shook with fear. Never before had he been so close to possible death.

"Let's go, Mr. Henry," called Kobe. "It's gone and I don't think it'll follow us."

Walt felt the perspiration roll down his face. The truck moved as fast as possible down the rough African road. When he knew they were out of danger, Ngoro broke the silence.

"We're very fortunate, Mr. Henry. That leopard was determined to fight, and some of us could have been killed back there."

"You're right, Ngoro. I would have shot him had he not moved but maybe that could have been even worse. What if I had only wounded him more?"

"Well, the Lord took care of us," replied Ngoro. "I don't even want to think what could have happened."

Walt smiled, "I never thought that as a missionary I would be called upon to defend the lives of you men from a leopard."

"I guess that's all in a day's work for a missionary, Mr. Henry," answered Kobe. "We'll never forget what you did for us. You have proven your love for us in many ways."

Kobe's words brought a lump to the missionary's throat.

"Another thing," chuckled Walt, "I never thought I would be riding on a log for a main spring either."

Ngoro looked over at his white friend. "Like Kobe said, Mr. Henry, it's all part of being a missionary. It's not just preaching the Word, but the practical everyday living of it, too."

"I guess you're right, Ngoro," replied the American.

As the pickup traveled on into the night, Walt Henry thanked the Lord repeatedly, in his heart, for his African family.